A
FIGHT
TO THE
DEATH

Strength for Life

Down, but Not Out: How to Get Up
When Life Knocks You Down

Humility: The Forgotten Virtue

A Fight to the Death: Taking Aim at Sin Within

A
FIGHT
TO THE
DEATH

Taking Aim at Sin Within

WAYNE A. MACK

AND

JOSHUA MACK

P&R PUBLISHING
P.O. BOX 817 • PHILLIPSBURG • NEW JERSEY 08865-0817

Unless otherwise indicated, Scripture quotations are from the *NEW AMERICAN STANDARD BIBLE*®. © Copyright 1960, 1962, 1963, 1968, 1971, 1972, 1973, 1975, 1977, 1995 by The Lockman Foundation. Used by permission. (www.Lockman.org)

Italics within Scripture quotations indicate emphasis added.

Page design by Kirk DouPonce, Dog Eared Design
Typesetting by Lakeside Design Plus

Printed in the United States of America

Library of Congress Cataloging-in-Publication Data

Mack, Wayne A.
    A fight to the death : taking aim at sin within / Wayne A. Mack and Joshua Mack.
        p. cm. — (Strength for life)
    Includes bibliographical references and index.
    ISBN-13: 978-1-59638-004-2 (pbk.)
    ISBN-10: 1-59638-004-7 (pbk.)
    1. Sin—Christianity. 2. Spiritual warfare. I. Mack, Joshua. II. Title.

BV4625.M32 2006
241'.3—dc22

2005052132

With heartfelt appreciation this book is dedicated to Roger and Geraldene Irwin, a brother and sister who have encouraged us in our ministries in numerous ways and who have for many years faithfully fought the good fight of faith described in this book.

We also dedicate this book to Harold Irwin Jr., who has now graduated to glory, but who was the person God used to lay the foundation of solid biblical truth in Wayne Mack's life when he was a young Christian.

CONTENTS

Foreword   9

Introduction   13

Part 1: Why Fight Sin?
1. Think about This   17
2. Know Your Enemy   24
3. The World's Worst Tyrant   33
4. Dumb and Dumber   42
5. If It's So Bad, Why Do I Feel So Good?   51

Part 2: How to Put Sin to Death
6. What Killing Your Sin Means   69
7. You Can Kill Your Sin Because . . .   82
8. Remember, You Don't Sin Alone   92
9. Pay Attention to the Seasons   105
10. You Must Know Yourself   116
11. Don't Listen to Sin's Sales Pitch   131
12. Learn from Failures   144
13. Concluding Lessons on Killing Sin   154

Notes   170

Index of Scripture   173

FOREWORD

The title of this valuable book, *A Fight to the Death*, may not typify titles in the popular evangelical literature of our day, but it accurately summarizes one of the most crucial doctrines of Christian living. At first glance, it may seem like a better title for the next action movie than for one of the most helpful books any Christian could read. Furthermore, it is likely that the premises of this book will *not* readily appeal to a great number of readers and churches who have fallen into self-seeking or seeker-driven perspectives. And yet, this book is the very thing that every soul desperately needs. Using passages like Matthew 5:27–30, Romans 8:13, and Colossians 3:5, Dr. Wayne Mack and Joshua Mack highlight and clearly develop the doctrine of *the mortification of sin*. This doctrine may sound scary, but my best advice to you, the reader, is not to let any apprehension deter you from this life-enriching study.

Not understanding and applying God's truth concerning our need to deal forthrightly with our sin nature is disastrous (James 1:12–15). This has been borne out in my own life, as I was influenced in Bible college to just "let go and let God" grow me. I know what it is to struggle with sin and not see much progress. You see, I was under the erroneous impression that if I could just *surrender* more, I would glide euphorically into godliness. Oh, how wrong I was. Surrendering is only the beginning place for the biblical process of change, growth, and regular victory that God has outlined in His Word (Rom. 12:1–2; cf. 1 Tim. 4:7–9).

As Puritans such as John Owen and Thomas Watson taught many years ago, there is no living the Christian life without a high view of God, a true hatred of sin, and a fervor to subdue the flesh by the grace of God (1 Peter 1:13–16). These writers often humbly let us in on their own battles against sin. They truly understood the Christian life and thus both glorified their God and left us a great pattern to follow. Like them, each one of us relying on the Spirit's empowering must be aware of the battle, get in it, and stay in it if we are to become more like Christ and know His joy.

As I counsel individuals and teach students at the college and seminary level, I see the need for this very type of book to assist in the learning process. After many years of ministering to God's people, I find that there is still a great need to deal with erroneous perspectives of sanctification (becoming more like Christ), such as the one with which I began my own Christian walk. Time and time again I must teach what the Scriptures have to say about the *real* Christian life. Having had the privilege of learning from and ministering together with Wayne, and having Joshua in my classes, I had no doubt that I could count on their book as a resource that I could wholeheartedly recommend to church members, counselees, and students. Not only do Wayne and Joshua present a thoroughly biblical approach to this much-needed teaching, they build the reader's understanding of this crucial doctrine step by step. The book is divided into two main sections: "Why Fight Sin?" and "How to Put Sin to Death." These sections offer practical help and illustrate the various lessons with examples that apply to everyday life.

If, in picking up this book, you were looking for a major catalyst for the Christian life—you have found it. Maybe you were looking for something to help a friend who is in need of what I have described. Perhaps you picked it up out of sheer curiosity. Whatever the case, may God bless you as you dare to investigate and use the truth found here. It will no doubt ultimately lead to a more strengthened, fruitful, and liberating path heavenward (Ps. 119:45; 2 Peter 1:5–11).

Stuart W. Scott
Associate Professor of Biblical Counseling
at Southern Seminary
Professor of Biblical Counseling at Boyce College
Fellow and Board Member of National Association
of Biblical Counselors

INTRODUCTION

Were you surprised by the title of this book? Did you think *A Fight to the Death* was a bit melodramatic? If so, we encourage you to read Romans 8:13 because the title of this book is really another way of stating the truth of that verse in a very straightforward way. It is essentially what Paul meant when he said: "If you are living according to the flesh, *you must die*; but if by the Spirit *you are putting to death* the deeds of the body, you will live." Our title is also a restatement of the truth found in Colossians 3:5, where believers are commanded: "Therefore *consider the members of your earthly body as dead* to immorality, impurity, passion, evil desire, and greed, which amounts to idolatry." Following that command, we are reminded of the importance of obedience and the seriousness of not putting sin to death: "For it is because of these things that the wrath of God will come upon the sons of disobedience" (Col. 3:6). In other words, failing to put sin to death is serious business. The apostle Paul was saying that either we destroy sin or it will destroy us.

Some time ago, a friend of mine told me about a man who introduced himself to a group as a hired killer. As you can imagine, the other people in the group were quite shocked (and perhaps a bit uneasy) to have someone in their midst who was so bold in announcing to the world that he was a hired killer. Fortunately, their concern was eliminated as the man went on to explain that he worked for a company that exterminated insect and animal pests.

According to the Bible, every believer should devote himself to being a killer—not of people or animal pests, but of sin. Put sin to death or it will destroy you and others. We write this book out of the biblical conviction that continuing in sin is a serious and dangerous matter. It is a foolish thing to mock or make light of sin (Prov. 14:9). We write this book also out of the conviction that true believers hate sin and want to overcome it (Eph. 2:10; Titus 2:7–11; 3:8). Finally, we write this book out of the conviction that true believers will want to put sin to death.

We understand that killing sin is not a means of earning or winning our salvation, which is always by the grace of God and based solely on the redemption that is freely given us in Christ Jesus (Rom. 3:24–25; Eph. 1:7; 2:8–9; Titus 3:5–6). Rather, we want to put sin to death because Christ "gave Himself for us to redeem us from every lawless deed, and to purify for Himself a people for His own possession, zealous for good deeds" (Titus 2:14).

Because of these convictions, in the first part of this book we will explore why sin is so serious and why we should fight against it. In the second part, we will present a biblical method for killing the sin within us.

Part 1

WHY
FIGHT
SIN?

1

THINK ABOUT THIS

"Hate evil, you who love the LORD. . . ." (Ps. 97:10)

I will always remember a little old grandma who heard that I was studying to be a pastor and wanted to give me a bit of advice before I headed off to serve at my first church. "Whatever you do," she said, "don't talk about sin. I used to go to a church where the pastor always talked about sin. It made me miserable. But the pastor of the church I go to now never talks about sin, and I love it." Sadly, her attitude is not all that unusual. Many people just love not talking about sin.

That is a problem. It is a problem because God's attitude toward the subject of sin is far different from that little old grandma's attitude. To God, talking about sin is important. It is so important that if a person does not get what God has to say about sin, he will not get anything else.

I realize that this is blunt, but it is the truth. Under-standing what the Bible teaches about sin is essential to understanding what the Bible teaches about everything else. And if we do not understand what the Bible teaches about sin, we certainly will not be able to understand God. In particular, we will never be able to figure out what He is so angry about.

I remember during my first year of college that I doubted God as I never had before. I had a difficult time coming to terms with His judgment on sin: a man put out his hand to steady the ark and he was struck dead; Moses got angry and he was not allowed to enter the Promised Land; and Adam and Eve ate some fruit and the whole world was sentenced to judgment. After a year's worth of struggle, I finally figured out what the problem was, and it was not with God. It was with me. I did not think sin was as bad as it really is, and as a result, I could not understand how right God's wrath really is.

Besides not being able to understand God, if we do not understand what the Bible teaches about sin, we will never be able to understand ourselves. If we want to figure out why we get angry, why we are selfish, why we treat people the way we do, why we have problems in our relationships, or why we are depressed, it is not enough to curl up on a couch and have a good cry. We have to understand what the Bible has to say about sin!

To take it a step further, we have to understand what the Bible teaches about sin in order to understand the world itself. Scattered across the globe are scholars, philosophers, and activists who are all trying to identify the source of our problems in the world today. They usually blame the world's problems on circumstances, economic conditions, poor parenting, or a lack of education. After years of research, they tell us things like: "Want to stop war? Make the nations prosperous." Or: "Want to wipe out crime in the inner city? Make sure kids get a proper education." Sorry, but these kinds of solutions do not cut it. They fall far short because they fail to deal with the root of the problem. They do not take into consideration what the Bible teaches about sin.

Quite frankly, the Bible will be one long, confusing book if we do not understand sin. Salvation, God's judgment, hell, heaven, death, punishment, justification, propitiation, and redemption make no sense apart from sin.

Considering that, what doctrine might Satan want to attack most? It is no surprise that Satan is relentless in his attack on what the Bible teaches about sin. By simply tampering with the doctrine of sin, he is able to make chaos of the Christian faith. If he can get us to think erroneously or even superficially about sin, he has us where he wants us. He knows that if we have a wrong understanding of sin, we will have a wrong understanding of everything else.

I am convinced that many problems in the church today can be traced back to a wrong understanding of sin. Churches are filled with individuals who are self-righteous and who are trusting in their own good works for salvation. Many people believe they are Christians because they are nice people, because they grew up in a Christian family, or because they go to church. Why is this? It is because they do not have any idea of the seriousness of their sin. If they could understand sin's seriousness, they would also quickly understand the folly of trusting for salvation in being baptized, going to church, or being born into a Christian family.

Our churches are filled with Christians who are not growing spiritually. Show me a Christian who is not growing, and I will show you a person who does not take sin seriously. Many people say that they want to grow, but really do not mean it—at least not enough. Mostly, they just like to say they want to grow. That way they can appear to be holy while continuing to indulge in the very things that keep them from being holy. They like the benefits of a godly life, but they do not want to make the sacrifices required in order to experience those benefits. They want to be godly, but they do not *really* want to be godly. They love their sin too much, and they will not deal with it until they grieve over it.

Although every true Christian has, at one point in his life, at least caught a glimpse of the seriousness of sin, it is easy to forget just how terrible it really is as we continue in our Christian walk. When that begins to happen, we can be sure that we have wandered far from God; for the more we get to know God, the more we will hate sin. When men see God for who He really is, they see themselves for who they really are. And when they see themselves for who they really are, their cry is the same: "Woe is me!"

Think about Paul as he grew in his Christian life. Early on, he wrote: "For I am the least of the apostles . . ." (1 Cor. 15:9). Later, he identified himself as "the very least of all saints" (Eph. 3:8). Finally, toward the very end of his life, he concluded: "Christ Jesus came into the world to save sinners, among whom I am foremost of all" (1 Tim. 1:15). The closer Paul got to the Light, the more the darkness of his heart was exposed.

It is certainly not the most pleasant experience in the world to have the darkness of our own hearts exposed. If we are willing to turn on the light of God's Word, however, we will see things about Jesus Christ that we have never seen before. When we think of ourselves adoringly, we think of Christ sparingly. But when we stop boasting in ourselves and begin to admit the truth about us, we become smaller in our own eyes and Christ becomes greater and more precious to us.

I appreciate how Charles Spurgeon once put it:

There are some professing Christians who can speak of themselves in terms of admiration; but, from my inmost heart, I loathe such speeches more and more every day that I live. Those who talk in such a boastful fashion must be constituted very differently from me. While they are congratulating themselves, I have to lie humbly at the foot of Christ's Cross, and marvel that I am saved at all, for I know that I am saved. I have to wonder that I do not believe Christ more, and equally wonder that I am privileged to believe in Him at all—to wonder that I do not love Him more, and equally to wonder that I am not holier, and equally to wonder that I have any desire to be holy at all considering what a polluted, debased, depraved nature I find still within my soul, notwithstanding all that divine grace has done in me. If God were ever to allow the fountains of the great deeps of depravity to break up in the best man that lives, he would make as bad a devil as the devil himself is. I care nothing for what these boasters say concerning their own perfections; I feel sure that they do not know themselves, or they could not talk as they often do. There is tinder enough in the saint who is nearest to heaven to kindle another hell if God should but permit a spark to fall upon it. In the very best of men there is an infernal and well-nigh infinite depth of depravity. Some Christians never seem to find this out. I almost wish that they might not do so, for it is a painful discovery for anyone to make; but it has the beneficial effect of making us cease from trusting in ourselves, and causing us to glory only in the Lord.[1]

I hope it is starting to become clear why it is so important for us to take a good, long, hard look at what the Bible teaches about sin. Before we can talk about overcoming it, we must see it for what it is. Doing this will not be easy. It will be uncomfortable. But it will be worth it! For by understanding the seriousness of sin, we will be better able to understand the greatness of God, the wonders of His grace, the beauty of Jesus Christ, and the process of sanctification.

APPLICATION AND DISCUSSION SUGGESTIONS

1. How would you describe our culture's attitude toward the subject of sin?

2. What are some reasons why it is important to understand what the Bible says about sin?

3. Describe several specific ways that a wrong understanding of sin affects other areas of a person's spiritual life.

4. What can we learn from the apostle Paul's attitude toward his sinfulness as he grew in his Christian life?

5. Why do you think it is easy to forget how terrible sin really is?

6. What happens to us spiritually when we forget how terrible our sin really is? Give specific examples from Scripture.

7. What commitment should you make as a result of what you have learned from this chapter?

2

KNOW YOUR ENEMY

"Everyone who practices sin also practices lawlessness; and sin is lawlessness." (1 John 3:4)

They say that ignorance is bliss. That may be true when it comes to knowing how many calories are in an ice-cream cone, but when it comes to things that are really important, ignorance is dangerous. Ignorance is certainly dangerous when it comes to the subject of sin. One of the reasons we play with sin is that we are ignorant about how dangerous it is. To make matters worse, we are ignorant about how ignorant we are about sin. We know sin is bad, but the way that we live makes it clear that we do not know how terrible it really is.

I know this is true from personal experience. One of the primary reasons I was motivated to look more carefully at what the Bible teaches about sin is my realization that, even as a pastor who spent hours in God's Word almost every day, I had an attitude toward sin that was slipping, and it scared me.

I could blame society for that. The world gets mad at us for trying to convert them, when in fact they are even more desperately trying to convert us. They want us to think the way they do. In particular, the world wants us to think the way they do about sin. Sometimes it seems as if our culture preaches a one-point evangelistic sermon: sin is not all that serious. The main goal on many popular television shows appears to be to show that sin is funny, not awful. Considering the world's aggressive, pro-sin agenda, if we are not careful we can become desensitized to sin. What God calls evil can slowly begin to appear normal—even good.

I could blame sin itself. Sin is deceptive. It wears masks. It is an ugly beast, but when it comes knocking on the door of our hearts, it is dressed up like a Girl Scout. It wants us to think that it wants only to sell us some cookies, when in fact it really wants to destroy us. We have to learn to rip off the disguises sin puts on in order to see how awful it really is.

But the main reason we do not hate sin the way we should is that our own hearts lie to us, as Jeremiah 17:9 points out: "The heart is more deceitful than all else and is desperately sick; who can understand it?" We deceive ourselves into believing that we are better than we really are.

The twisted thing is that most of us can see that other people's sin is terrible. We even do a good job of exposing sin in others. But when it comes to our own sin, we are even better at ignoring it. This kind of thing happens all the time: a parent screams at a child for screaming at his sister; a wife refuses to talk to her husband because she thinks he is being selfish; a person gossips about someone she thinks has offended her.

It is sad to meet a person who has been deceived by someone else, but it is even more tragic to meet a person who is deceiving himself. Yet too often, that is exactly what many of us are doing with the sin in our lives. As one writer put it, when it comes to our own sin, "we deny . . . what we know to be true. We assert . . . what we know to be false. We prettify ugly realities and sell ourselves the prettified versions. . . . We become our own dupes."[1]

One reason we fall into this trap is that we have only a vague understanding of what sin is. Perhaps that is why the authors of Scripture go to such great lengths to define and describe it. The variety of terms the Bible uses for sin is pretty amazing (more than seventeen distinct terms are used in Scripture). God has a purpose for giving us such vivid descriptions of sin. It is to keep us from being deceived by the world, by sin, and by our own hearts. He wants us to see sin for what it really is!

Sin Is Rebellion

Sin is any failure to conform to God's holy law. We are talking here about both action and attitude. The apostle John put it like this: "sin is lawlessness" (1 John 3:4). Therefore, we sin when we do, say, or think anything that God commands us not to. Likewise, we sin when we do not do, say, or think what God commands us to. The slightest departure from absolute obedience to God's law is sin.

This is why sin is often described as a "transgression." The word *transgression* literally means to revolt or rebel against a rightful authority. When we think about sin, we tend to think horizontally; in other words, we tend to think about our relationships with people. We need to understand, however, that all sin is ultimately vertical. All sin is against God. That is why, after committing adultery and even murder, David cried out to God, "Against You, You only, I have sinned" (Ps. 51:4). It is not that David did not sin against Bathsheba and Uriah, but that the person most offended by his sin was God.

When we sin, we are shaking our fists at God. We are treating a good and gracious God as if He were our worst enemy; we are warring against Him. Worse, we are acting like a traitor. Imagine an American hiding Osama bin Laden in his house, taking him out to dinner, going to local amusement parks, and treating him as if he were a good friend. If a person acted like that, without a doubt, he would be called a traitor. Yet when we hide sin in our hearts, that is exactly what we are doing with God. We are committing treason. We are betraying God and even ourselves.

SIN IS PERVERSION

A pervert is not merely someone who sits up in his room looking at dirty pictures. To *pervert* something literally means to twist or distort it. And that is exactly what we do when we sin. We twist and distort something that is good into something that is not. We are being perverted.

Take sexual sin, for example. God has a great plan for sex, a plan that, when followed, brings joy and satisfaction. But people sin by taking what God designed for their good and twisting it into something awful, something that brings them momentary pleasure but lasting harm. Or think about idolatry. God designed us to worship Him. When we worship someone or something other than God, we are being perverted. We are taking that which is right (worshiping God) and twisting it into something evil (worshiping someone else).

Our problems often stem from good desires that are improperly directed. Take a young man who wants to do well in school. There is certainly nothing wrong with wanting to excel. But this young man allows that desire to become an obsession, and suddenly doing well in school becomes his chief objective in life. What has happened? He has perverted that which was good and made it sin. Or consider a young lady who wants to have a boyfriend. Again, that desire, in and of itself, is not wrong. But if she allows that desire to dominate her and is willing to compromise what she knows to be true and right in order to achieve it, she is being perverted.

SIN IS EMPTINESS

When we choose to sin, we choose to do something that is inherently ineffective. In the long run, sin does not work. That is why when the Old Testament writers saw someone sinning, they would sometimes say he was doing "emptiness."

Sinning is like getting into a bathtub filled with water, grabbing the sides, and then trying to lift the bathtub to the ceiling. Obviously, this would result in nothing more than wasted energy because it is ultimately pointless to even attempt such a thing. Likewise, the sinner chases after the wind, pursuing something he will never catch. As the apostle Paul noted, what he is doing is futile (Eph. 4:17).

SIN IS BREAKING A TRUST

Sin is often called unfaithfulness. In the Bible, the word for *unfaithfulness* is the same word used for *adultery*. Sinning against God is committing spiritual adultery.

The prophet Ezekiel was pretty graphic. He said that when God's people sinned, they were acting like prostitutes: "But you trusted in your beauty and played the harlot because of your fame, and you poured out your harlotries on every passer-by who might be willing" (Ezek. 16:15). We like to trivialize sin, but we need to understand that when we sin against God, we are being like a prostitute. God has been faithful to us, but we choose to be unfaithful to Him. We are not only breaking God's laws, but violating a beautiful relationship.

SIN IS GETTING LOST

Biblically, we can choose to travel one of two paths through life: the path of godliness or the path of wickedness. When we obey God's law, we are walking in the path of godliness; and when we sin, we are walking in the path of wickedness.

The important thing to understand is that by sinning, we turn aside from the path God has laid out for us to follow. We are wandering off God's way. This means that we are crossing over boundaries He has set for our good and for our protection and trespassing in forbidden, dangerous territory.

Sin is more than doing what we want. It is doing the exact opposite of what God wants. It is doing that which God hates. That is why it is so often called an abomination to God. Sin is disgusting to God.

To take it a step further, when we sin we are doing what the devil desires. God hates sin; Satan loves it. So by sinning, we are doing what God hates and what Satan loves. Thomas Watson explained, "Sin gratifies Satan. When lust or anger burn in the soul, Satan warms himself at the fire. Men's sins feast the devil. . . . How he laughs to see people giving up their souls for the world, as if one should trade diamonds for straws. . . ."[2]

We have to see our sin for what it really is. When we sin, we are missing the mark and straying from the fold. We are acting like people who are spiritually blind and deaf. We are being unfaithful to our faithful God. We are committing spiritual adultery. We are doing the very thing that God hates.

We point out all of this because when we are tempted, we will always desire to minimize the seriousness of our sin. Satan, the world, and our own hearts will tell us that sin is not that bad. But we must respond by speaking the truth about sin to ourselves. If we do not, we are placing ourselves in great danger because lying to ourselves about the threat of sin does not at all change the magnitude of the threat itself.

A little more than a hundred years ago, in May 1902, a volcano on the island of Martinique was beginning to concern the residents of the city of Saint-Pierre. Unfortunately, the volcano was heating up in an election year. The governor of Martinique was worried that if too much attention was given to the volcano, the candidates of his party would suffer in the upcoming election. So he went to work.

He told the editor of a local paper to minimize stories focusing on the danger of an eruption. He stopped people from sending telegrams that warned of the threat. He even visited the city himself several days before the election just so that people knew things were safe. As it happened, the day after he arrived in Saint-Pierre, the volcano erupted. It ended up killing the governor and thirty thousand other people in less than two minutes.

Satan, the world, and our own flesh often downplay the seriousness of sin in the same way that the governor tried to downplay the seriousness of that volcano. Let us not fool ourselves. Sin is our enemy, and it wants to destroy us.

APPLICATION AND DISCUSSION SUGGESTIONS

1. What are some reasons that it is very easy to minimize the seriousness of sin?

2. Describe some specific ways that you have been tempted by the world to minimize the seriousness of sin.

3. What are some different disguises that sin wears to make itself look more attractive than it really is?

4. How do we lie to ourselves about the seriousness of sin? What are some ways that you have lied to yourself about specific sins in the past?

5. What specific step can you take to keep yourself from being deceived by sin?

6. What difference should knowing that all sin is vertical make in your attitude toward it?

7. Why is sin perverted? Can you give specific illustrations of how sin perverts things?

8. How is sinning against God acting like an adulterer?

9. What changes do you need to make in your life as a result of what you have studied in this chapter? What are you going to do to make those changes happen?

3

THE WORLD'S WORST
TYRANT

"For the wages of sin is death. . . ." (Rom. 6:23)

It amazes me how fast my ten-month-old daughter can crawl around the house. I love watching her because she is so focused and fast. But no matter where she is headed or how much of a hurry she is in, there is one place where she is always careful: the steps. She will crawl right over to the step, look down, shake her head no, and then put her hands up in the air because she wants me to pick her up. I wish I could take credit for teaching her that, but I cannot. She learned to be careful the hard way, after falling on her face as she tried to crawl down a step in the kitchen.

It does not take long for us to figure out that actions have consequences. My daughter is not even a year old and she is starting to understand this. Unfortunately, while most people understand that this is true when it comes to their physical lives, not nearly as many people understand that this is spiritually true as well.

I am not sure why this is so hard for us to get. After all, it is not as if the Bible fails to go to great lengths to make it clear. The apostle Paul explained, "Do not be deceived, God is not mocked; for whatever a man sows, this he will also reap. For the one who sows to his own flesh will from the flesh reap corruption, but the one who sows to the Spirit will from the Spirit reap eternal life" (Gal. 6:7–8). Apparently, even believers are easily fooled into believing that they can think however they want to think, say whatever they want to say, and do whatever they want to do, and these things will have no spiritual effect on them.

We have all experienced this lie. "I can be best friends with a person who hates God and it won't affect me at all." "I can go a long time without studying God's Word and still be a strong believer." "I can watch whatever I want to watch and it won't change me." When people say things like that, it indicates that they are living in a fantasy world because in the real world, choices have consequences. That is why Paul said, "Do not be deceived. You reap what you sow." In other words, when we sin we will suffer.

Fortunately, the Bible is very specific about the consequences of choosing to sin. God's Word tells us very clearly what sin produces. When we are tempted to disobey God, we do not have to wonder what the result will be if we give in.

Sin is filthy. That is why when the Bible talks about being holy, it talks about being clean, and when it talks about sinning, it talks about defiling oneself. When someone rolls around in the mud, his body gets dirty, and when someone rolls around in sin, his soul gets dirty.

In Zechariah 3:3, Joshua the high priest is pictured standing before the angel of the Lord, clothed in filthy garments. Those filthy garments represent sin. We know that because in the very next verse, the angel says that by removing the filthy garments from Joshua, he has taken Joshua's iniquity away.

This is a very helpful picture. Imagine waking up one day and going to the closet to decide what to wear. Hanging in the closet are two choices: a beautiful, clean outfit (representing holiness) and an outfit covered with cow manure (representing sin). When we sin, we are choosing to put on the outfit covered with cow manure. We might be tempted to think that this is an overly graphic picture of sin, but it is really not graphic enough. Sin is so dirty that God compares it to blood, wounds, sores, scum, leprosy, and other awful diseases. It makes sense that one old Puritan called sin "the plague of plagues."

In Matthew 23:27–28 Jesus compared sin to the inside of a tomb. Think about what it would be like to open up a coffin after it had been in the ground for a while and see a body rotting away inside. It would be revolting. Yet that is exactly what Jesus said the soul of a person who has a regular pattern of sin in his life looks like.

I think Solomon really got the point across in Proverbs 26:11 when he compared sin to vomit: "Like a dog that returns to its vomit is a fool who repeats his folly." *Folly* is another biblical word for *sin*. So when we think about sinning, we need to think about vomit. We can just picture entering our living room and seeing our dog licking up its vomit. If we saw our dog doing that, we would want to cover our eyes or make him stop. Yet that is what we do when we choose to continue in our sin. We are being like that dog. We are enjoying vomit.

To be as blunt as possible: sin makes us ugly. As one writer explains, "Sin is to the soul what rust is to gold, what scars are to a beautiful face, what stain is to white silk cloth. It is ugliness across the face of beauty. . . ."[1] Sin distorts and disfigures the inner man. Whether we are talking about what the world considers a small sin or a great one, sin is disgusting the whole way around. "Sin is a poison, sinners serpents; sin is called vomit, sinners dogs; sin is called the stench of graves, sinners rotten sepulchers; sin is called mire, sinners pigs. Sin is defiling, degrading. It stamps the devil's image on the human soul."[2]

OUR SIN WILL MAKE IT EASIER
FOR US TO SIN SOME MORE

Every small sin wants to be a big sin when it grows up. That is why Paul admonishes his readers in Romans 13:14 to "make no provision for the flesh in regard to its lusts." If we give sin an inch, it will take a mile, so we must not allow our flesh any leeway in regard to its lusts. Al Martin writes:

Sin comes to us with modest proposals. "Indulge me this little bit. . . . But the child of God never forgets sin's real intentions. Every stirring of envy, if it had its way, would lead to murder and destruction. Every doubt of any phrase of Scripture, if it had its way, would lead to the ultimate denial of God and of every truth of Scripture. Every breathing of pride in its first stirrings, if it had its way, would run and tear the crown off God's head. . . . Strike at the first risings of sin! Sin's proposals are modest, and if you once let them gain ground in your affections, it will then go to the judgment and it will lessen your ability to grapple with it. Never debate with passions. Passion has never lost a debate yet. The most powerful persuasive debater is sinful passion leading to envy, uncleanness, to doubt, to pride. "Ah, isn't that a bit morbid and a bit extreme?" says someone. I answer, look at the great train of people who like Samson, once knew what it was to accomplish mighty conquests for God but who now have their eyes out and are chained to some mill and they grind out day after day an empty, powerless, useless round of "Christian" activity—I put "Christian" in quotes. The breath of the Almighty has gone from their lives. Where did it start? When sin came in with a little modest proposal, and the door was opened, and sin was entertained. Strike at the first risings of sin![3]

If we do not strike at the first risings of sin, we are going to end up going places and doing things that we never thought we would!

Sin once and it becomes more difficult not to sin in the future. When we choose to sin, it is as if we are choosing to push a ball down a hill. Our sin is going to pick up speed and it is going to become more and more difficult to stop.

This is made obvious by the fact that people hardly ever commit single sins. Consider a child who is irresponsible and thus does not do his homework. As a result, he is not ready to take a test. Since he is not ready to take the test, he is tempted to cheat. Under pressure, he gives in. But he cheats off someone who is not well prepared either, so he gets a poor grade. He knows his parents want him to do his best, so when the teacher gives him the graded test to take home, he is tempted to hide it. He throws the test away on the way home. After a while, the teacher figures out what happened and calls the parents. His parents confront the child and he lies about it. They get so angry about his lying that they ground him for a month, and he gets so angry about being grounded that he runs away.

Sin messes everything up. This is just one illustration; we could easily think of many more. It is easy to see why the writer of Hebrews says that we should lay aside "the sin which so easily entangles us" (Heb. 12:1). Sin is a trap. When we do it, we are in great danger of getting stuck.

Paul makes the same point from a different angle in Ephesians 4:26–27. He was talking about a specific sin, but the principle holds true for sin in general. "Be angry, and yet do not sin; do not let the sun go down on your anger. . . ." Paul was telling Christians that they must be very careful about how they deal with anger. They must deal with it quickly. Why? Because there is a great danger: "do not give the devil an opportunity." If they fail to deal with their anger correctly, the devil will use that as an opportunity to take advantage of them.

It is critical for us to understand that when we indulge in sin, we give the devil a chance to lead us down a path we ought not to tread. This means that if we are telling ourselves that our sin is small and that we can handle it, we are fooling ourselves. That small sin does not want to stay a small sin, and by giving in we are giving the devil an opportunity to wreak havoc in our lives. When we give in to sin, it is as if we were handing a teenager the key to our house and saying, "I'm going away on vacation; why don't you come over while I'm away—and by the way, please wreck my house!"

THE WORLD'S WORST TYRANT

Saddam Hussein, the infamous former Iraqi dictator, has nothing on sin. Sin is, as Charles Spurgeon used to say, "the world's worst tyrant." If someone sat down and wrote the story of all the suffering that people have experienced at the hands of tyrants throughout the history of the world, it would be too terrible to read. But even all the suffering inflicted by evil tyrants could never compare to the suffering men have experienced as a result of their own sin.

As Spurgeon went on to explain:

Sin has brought more plagues upon this earth than all the earth's tyrants. It has brought more pangs and more miseries upon men's bodies and souls than the craftiest inventions of the most cold-blooded . . . tormentors. Sin . . . is such a tyranny that none but those whom God delivers have been able to escape from it. Nay, such a tyranny that even they have been scarcely saved; and they, when saved, have had to look back and remember the dreadful slavery in which they once existed.[4]

Sin does not want to lift us up; sin wants to bring us down. Sin does not want to help us; sin wants to destroy us. Sin is warring against us (1 Peter 2:11). So do not be fooled when temptation comes. Sin is our enemy, not our friend.

This chapter has described just two of the ways that this terrible tyrant tortures its slaves. The list goes on and on. Sin can make a person physically sick (Ps. 32:3–4). Sin brings shame (Prov. 11:2). Sin hinders prayer (1 Peter 3:7). Sin squelches a believer's desire for the Word (1 Peter 2:1–2). Sin hurts not only the person sinning, but also the people around him, and it makes it easier for them to sin (Prov. 22:24–25; 1 Tim. 5:22). Sin has no mercy. It laughs at our pain and delights in our misery. Sin makes Hitler look good.

It is no fun to talk about a tyrant. It is not enjoyable to think about torture. And it can be difficult to look directly at what the Bible says about sin. It is a little bit like looking at a picture of a murder victim: we cringe and want to turn away and think happier thoughts. But although it is uncomfortable, it is extremely important that we come face to face with just how awful sin is. This is one unpleasant task that is absolutely necessary for the good of our souls. If we are going to avoid being enticed by the lies that sin tells us, we must learn to fix the consequences of sin in our minds so that we can think straight when temptation threatens to cloud our judgment.

APPLICATION AND DISCUSSION SUGGESTIONS

1. What does Galatians 6:7–8 teach us about our spiritual life and the way we think about sin?

2. What are some specific examples of past ways in which sin has fooled you about its consequences?

3. What does the fact that God compares sin to blood, wounds, sores, scum, leprosy, and other awful diseases teach us about the nature of sin?

4. How does sin make us ugly? What are some ways in which you have found this to be true in your own life?

5. What tends to happen when a person does not "strike at the first risings of sin"? Why?

6. What does the fact that people hardly ever commit single sins teach you about the nature of sin?

7. What are some of the other consequences of sin that this chapter does not discuss? Give examples from Scripture of the consequences of sin.

8. Why is it important to force yourself to think about the consequences of sin?

9. What specific sin in your life are you minimizing the consequences of? How are you going to deal with that sin differently as a result of what you have now learned?

4

DUMB AND DUMBER

"Fools mock at sin. . . ." (Prov. 14:9)

Sinning is always stupid. Or, to use a more biblical term, sinning is always foolish. We are not sinning every time we do something stupid, but we do something stupid every time we sin. Every time we break God's law and every time we fail to do what God desires, we are hurting ourselves and we are doing something that is fundamentally foolish. Whether it is a wrong thought, a wrong word, or a wrong action, sin is not only disobedience—sin is dumb.[1]

Those statements, though bold, are not hard to prove. God's Word goes to great lengths to make it very clear that sinning is not smart.

THE WAY IT USED TO BE

Consider the way in which God describes what we were like before He saved us. If we look carefully at various biblical passages, we will find that not only does He say that we were rebelling against Him, He says that we were not even thinking clearly. Paul pounded this point home in Ephesians 4:17–19:

> So this I say, and affirm together with the Lord, that you walk no longer just as the Gentiles also walk, in the futility of their mind, being darkened in their understanding, excluded from the life of God because of the ignorance that is in them, because of the hardness of their heart; and they, having become callous, have given themselves over to sensuality for the practice of every kind of impurity with greediness.

Paul did not pull any punches, did he? The words he used to describe what we were like before God saved us are pretty graphic: we had a futile mind and a darkened understanding, and as a result we were spiritually ignorant. In other words, our problem was not just that our hearts were hard, but also that our minds were dark.

The unbeliever may be the most intelligent man in the world, but the fact that he chooses to disobey God and live in sin proves that when it comes to his relationship with God and spiritual things, he does not have a clue. He is like a man walking around in the dark. He is spiritually blind. The problem is, he will not admit it. He pretends that he can see when in fact he cannot.

Paul pinpointed unbelievers' real problem in Romans 1:18–23:

> For the wrath of God is revealed from heaven against all ungodliness and unrighteousness of men who sup-

press the truth in unrighteousness, because that which is known about God is evident within them; for God made it evident to them. For since the creation of the world His invisible attributes, His eternal power and divine nature, have been clearly seen, being understood through what has been made, so that they are without excuse. For even though they knew God, they did not honor Him as God or give thanks, but they became futile in their speculations, and their foolish heart was darkened. Professing to be wise, they became fools, and exchanged the glory of the incorruptible God for an image in the form of corruptible man and of birds and four-footed animals and crawling creatures.

That is a pretty pathetic picture. Men reject God and choose sin, claiming that what they are doing is intelligent and coming up with all sorts of elaborate rationalizations for their rebellion, when in fact, by rejecting God and choosing to sin, the only thing they are really becoming is more and more foolish.

When a person defends his sin and defends his rejection of God, he is somewhat like a child trying to explain how something complicated works. He mimics an adult, talks in a deep voice, and tries to sound all grown up and intelligent as he explains, "The engine goes *whir, whir*, and then the plane starts rolling. The wings shake, which help it lift off the ground, and all of a sudden you are flying. And that's the way it works." Not quite. The difference, of course, is that when a child talks like that, he is being fairly innocent, but when a sinner defends his sin, he is not innocent at all. He is suppressing the truth. That is exactly what we did before God saved us.

That is why one of the most common names for *sin* in Scripture is *folly*, and one of the most common names for *sinner* is *fool*. When we talk about someone doing something foolish, we are usually talking about someone making an innocent but unintelligent mistake. But when the Bible talks about someone doing something foolish, it is most often referring to someone rebelling against God.

For example, in Jeremiah 4:22, God rebuked His people, saying, "For My people are foolish . . . ; they are stupid children and have no understanding. They are shrewd to do evil, but to do good they do not know." The fact that they were so smart about sinning was proof that in reality they were foolish and lacked understanding.

It is interesting to note the way in which Jesus concluded the Sermon on the Mount: "Therefore everyone who hears these words of Mine and acts on them, may be compared to a wise man who built his house on the rock. . . . Everyone who hears these words of Mine and does not act on them, will be like a foolish man who built his house on the sand" (Matt. 7:24, 26).

Imagine driving along a neighborhood street and spotting a person who was trespassing on someone else's property in order to build a house for himself. We would say that what he was doing was wrong. But then, if we noticed that he was building that house on top of a sinkhole, it would cause us to add that what he was doing was not only wrong, but really stupid.

Jesus told another story in Luke 12 that is a bit more specific and helps to illustrate the point. He described a rich man whose land was very productive:

And he began reasoning to himself, saying, "What shall I do, since I have no place to store my crops?" Then he said, "This is what I will do: I will tear down my barns and build larger ones, and there I will store all my grain and my goods. And I will say to my soul, 'Soul, you have many goods laid up for many years to come; take your ease, eat, drink and be merry.' " (Luke 12:17–19)

What would most people in our world say about this man's life? "Are you kidding? He has it all! He is living the American dream." But what did God say about this man's life—about the American dream? "But God said to him, 'You fool! This very night your soul is required of you; and now who will own what you have prepared?' So is the man who stores up treasure for himself, and is not rich toward God" (Luke 12:20–21).

What did God call him? A fool. He was not only disobedient, not only greedy, and not only selfish, but also stupid. God looked on that man and the way he was living and said that it was a stupid way to live because he was completely missing the point. Am I going a little bit overboard, emphasizing this a bit too much? If it seems that I am just repeating myself, the book of Proverbs may be surprising. That entire book was basically written to make this one point.

Solomon wanted his son to be wise, so throughout the entire book of Proverbs he kept showing him what it looks like to be wise and what it looks like to be a fool. What does he say is at the root of it all? The wise person obeys God; the fool does not. *Wisdom* and *foolishness* are used throughout Proverbs virtually synonymously with *righteousness* and *unrighteousness*. If a person is being righteous, he is being wise. If a person is sinning, he is being foolish. The two cannot be separated.

The fool is not defined in terms of his mental intelligence, but rather by his attitude toward God and his attitude toward sin. In Proverbs 14:9, Solomon says, "Fools mock at sin." A foolish person does not take sin seriously. He laughs at it. Conversely, the wise man "is cautious and turns away from evil" (Prov. 14:16).

If we could ask Solomon to point out someone who was not very smart, he would not introduce us to someone who did poorly in school, who had a hard time reading or doing math. Instead, he would introduce us to someone who did not hate sin but delighted in it. We are not going out on a limb when we call sin folly. The two words are synonyms. The question is, however, what does the Bible mean when it characterizes sin as foolish? And what does the fact that God calls sin foolish tell us about the nature of sin?

Banging Your Head Against the Wall

To put it very simply, by calling sin foolish, the Bible is telling us that sin does not work. Proverbs 13:15 says that the way of the sinner "is hard." When the Bible says that sinning is foolish, it is saying that when a person sins, he is trying to push a square peg into a round hole. He is, as Cornelius Platinga puts it,

> using the wrong recipe for good health . . . the wrong gasoline to put in the tank . . . the wrong road to take

home. . . . To rebel against God is to saw off the branch that supports you . . . to flee from God to some far country to search for fulfillment there is to find only "black-market" substitutes. . . . Sin dissipates us into futile and self-destructive projects. Sin hurts other people and grieves God, but it also corrodes us. Sin is a form of self abuse.[2]

Biblical wisdom is practical, by and large. It is the ability to take what we know and use it in real-life situations. Wisdom is understanding the way life works and distinguishing between what is smart and what is not. It is being prudent, having discretion, and understanding what works and what does not.

The wise person "gets it." As he goes about living his life, he is not constantly bumping his head up against the wall. He knows how to solve the problems that come his way instead of simply making them worse. The fool, on the other hand, does not really "get it." He is thickheaded and dim-witted, and he does not understand the way God designed this world to work. As a result, he chooses to sin and makes one bad choice after another.

I recently read a story about the way in which President James Garfield died, and it illustrates the way that fools work. President Garfield set out for his college reunion in July 1881 and was shot down on the way by a lawyer who was upset about something the president had done.

Doctors spent eighty days trying to remove the bullet, but all they did was to make the problem worse. One doctor stuck a probe into the wound, which misled the other doctors. Then he stuck an unwashed finger into the wound, which caused the wound to become infected. Another doctor stuck his hand in wrist-deep and punctured President Garfield's liver. By poking and prodding, sixteen doctors turned a three-inch hole into a twenty-inch infected canal.

The president made it through that summer but died on September 14. Later, an autopsy revealed that the bullet was lodged in a spot that was not life-threatening. In other words, President Garfield would have lived if the doctors had left him alone. Their attempts to solve the problem only made it much, much worse. That is the fool. He always finds a way to make his problems worse.

Learn This Lesson Well

God has been very gracious to us. Since He is the Creator and we are His creatures, He could have simply said, "Do this" or "Do that," without giving us any reasons why. But instead, He showed mercy by going a step further and telling us not only what to do, but why. And one of the motivations He most frequently gives us is simply this: obedience is wise; disobedience is foolish.

We must do whatever we can to remember that principle. It is easy, while we are reading a book like this, to agree that sin is foolish; it is much more difficult to believe when we are being tempted to sin. The fact is, when we are tempted, sin often appears to be pretty smart. And that is exactly when we need to remember that sin is a liar. It is not telling us the truth. To sin is always stupid.

APPLICATION AND
DISCUSSION SUGGESTIONS

1. What does the Bible mean when it says that sinning is foolish?

2. What are some biblical illustrations of the foolishness of sin?

3. What does Romans 1:18–25 teach us about the folly of sin?

4. How is sin "self-abuse"?

5. What are some examples of the foolishness of sin from your own life?

6. What are some examples of times when sin has seemed wise to you?

7. How is what the Bible says about the folly of sin an example of God's grace?

8. Does sin usually seem foolish when you are being tempted?

9. What are some specific steps you can take to remember that sin is foolish when you are tempted to think that sinning is the best option to take?

5

IF IT'S SO BAD, WHY DO I FEEL SO GOOD?

"For it is because of these things that
the wrath of God will come. . . ." (Col. 3:6)

It is not difficult to prove how awful sin is biblically. It is not as if all of this teaching on sin were tucked away in some obscure, rarely read, dusty portion of the Old Testament. God makes it crystal clear throughout His Word: sin is disgusting. It is not even difficult to prove how awful sin is experientially. Sin has hurt every one of us. We have picked up the rattlesnake and we have been bitten by it. Yet in spite of the fact that we know sin hurts us and grieves God, we often play with it and sometimes even delight in it.

Why do we not hate that which wants to destroy us? We could answer that question in a number of different ways. It might be because we are not truly born again. Solomon said in Proverbs 8:13, "The fear of the LORD is to hate evil. . . ." If a person does not hate evil, he does not fear God, and if he does not fear God, he will not hate evil. Unbelievers, according to the apostle Paul, "walk, in the futility of their mind, being darkened in their understanding, excluded from the life of God because of the ignorance that is in them, because of the hardness of their heart; and they, having become callous, have given themselves over to sensuality . . ." (Eph. 4:17–19). They love sin because they are not converted.

Another reason might be a lack of faith in God. Even Christians can have weak faith. A person may not hate his sin because he does not fully believe that God is omniscient. He does not have an overwhelming awareness that God sees absolutely everything that he does. He soothes his conscience by fooling himself into thinking that he can hide certain sins from God.

Still another reason for not hating sin might be that a person thinks of himself as less of a sinner than he really is. Sometimes people have images of themselves that do not correspond with reality. If a person does not think he is much of a sinner, it is not because he is right; it is only because he is fooling himself into thinking that he is right. But if he has fooled himself into thinking that he is not much of a sinner, he will probably not take his sin very seriously.

I am sure there are many other reasons why we do not hate our sin the way we should. In this chapter, however, I want to zero in on the reason most frequently given in Scripture.

WE DON'T TAKE SIN SERIOUSLY BECAUSE WE DON'T TAKE GOD'S JUDGMENT SERIOUSLY

If a person is going to treat sin lightly, he must first refuse to take God's judgment seriously. When we understand that God's judgment on sin is absolutely right, that it is not too much or too little, and that His judgment on the smallest of sins is ultimately eternal death—meaning that the smallest deviation from His law, in God's eyes, is worthy of an eternity in hell—then we will understand how terrible it is to disobey God. When we begin to understand that God is not being harsh or unfair when He judges sin, we will begin to understand that sin is an awful, awful thing.

This is one reason why the prophets of God who called on His people to see their sin for what it was, grieve over it, confess it, and forsake it did not just tell the people to repent, but also told them why. And when the prophets explained why, they talked about God's judgment. They motivated men to take their sin seriously by reminding them that God's judgment was real.

To help us get a picture of how awful sin is, think about the awful judgment God has ordained for it. It is called hell. Hell is not a figment of someone's imagination. If we believe that the Bible is the Word of God, we must believe that there is a hell. It is difficult to speak and think about such a place, but it must be spoken of and thought about because it is a reality.

David wrote about hell. In Psalm 11:6, he said, "Upon the wicked He will rain snares of fire; fire and brimstone and burning wind will be the portion of their cup." Paul talked about hell. In 2 Thessalonians 1:7–9, he wrote that Jesus is going to come again and that when He does, He is going to deal out "retribution to those who do not know God and to those who do not obey the gospel of our Lord Jesus. These will pay the penalty of eternal destruction. . . ."

The apostle John spoke of hell. He prophesied in Revelation 20:15: "And if anyone's name was not found written in the book of life, he was thrown into the lake of fire." And Jesus taught about hell. He said in Matthew 5:30: "If your right hand makes you stumble, cut it off and throw it from you; for it is better for you to lose one of the parts of your body, than for your whole body to go into hell."

Hell is a real and horrifying place. In the words of one writer:

> There is no way to describe hell. Nothing on earth can compare with it. No living person has any real idea of it. No madman in wildest flights of insanity ever beheld its horror. No man in delirium ever pictured a place so utterly terrible as this. No nightmare racing across a fevered mind ever produces a terror to match that of the mildest hell. No murder scene with splashed blood and oozing wound ever suggested a revulsion that could touch the borderlands of hell. Let the most gifted writer exhaust his skill in describing

this roaring cavern of unending flame, and he would not even brush in fancy the nearest edge of hell.[1]

In His parables, Jesus often described it as a place of darkness (Matt. 8:12; 22:13; 25:30). He also described hell as a place where there will be weeping and gnashing of teeth—people screaming and writhing in anger and agony. He described it as a place of *eternal* fire. He said in Matthew 25:41 that on the judgment day, He will say to those who are on His left, "Depart from Me, accursed ones, into the eternal fire which has been prepared for the devil and his angels." In Matthew 13:41–42, He actually called it a furnace of fire.

Hell is a place of eternal pain. The word *eternal* is what makes the biblical picture of hell so terrifying. If there were an end to hell, there would be some hope. But there is no end, and in hell there is no hope.

While everyone suffers in hell, we know that the degrees of suffering in hell are different. Hebrews 10:29 says, "How much severer punishment do you think he will deserve who has trampled under foot the Son of God. . . ." If there were not degrees of suffering in hell, it would be impossible to say that one type of suffering was more severe. Hell is going to be horrible for everyone, but not everyone is going to be punished to the same extent. As one writer explained, "We can have absolute confidence that God, the righteous judge, will take absolutely everything into account. . . . Not one soul will be in hell who does not deserve to be; and no one's hell will be darker and deeper than what is right."

It is tempting to look at what the Bible says about hell and get upset with God because we think hell is too much and God is being unjust. But the reality is, *God is completely just, and therefore hell is completely right.* Hell is punishment. It is not as if God were up in heaven, delighting in the fact that He can torture people forever. That is not at all what hell is about. Hell is God's absolute justice on display.

Hell is God's justice on display because sin incurs guilt. To put it another way, hell is God's justice on display because sin is a crime. For God to be just, that sin must be punished. Under God's government, the punishment of every sin is inevitable. And the right punishment for sin is hell. There would not be a hell if there were not sin; and as one old Puritan explained, God is always fair, and hell's punishment will be absolutely just.

Just because a person does not think that what he has done is all that terrible, does not mean he is right. I recently read about a gang member who was arrested because he had shot someone in cold blood. When the police threatened him with prison time, he responded by saying that prison was no big deal because he needed to go to prison to get a street "rep." There was no remorse, no understanding of the significance of his crime.

When it comes to our sin, we often respond in the same way. We have no understanding of the significance of our crimes. When we get to heaven, we are going to see how awful sin is and we are going to see very clearly that the punishment sin deserves is hell. We are going to understand why sin deserves an eternity of rejection, sorrow, anguish, and pain. And we are going to see that judgment is not too much and not too little. It is just right because sin is that awful.

I am guessing that intellectually most of us are aware of this. But be warned that in thinking about hell, we, as religious people in particular, face a very subtle danger. The unbeliever does not believe in God's judgment, so he is not really concerned about his sin. But many religious people have a different problem. Though they believe in God's judgment, they have a hard time believing that their sin really deserves it.

Many believers divide up sin and sinners in their minds. There are "really big sins" that are "really bad," and the people who do them are "terrible sinners" who deserve God's judgment; and there are others, such as themselves, whose sin is not that serious. By dividing up sin and sinners like that, they are able to tell themselves that they believe in God's judgment while minimizing the seriousness of their own sin.

If we are going to hate sin and thus be motivated to deal with it, we need to believe that our own sin deserves eternal hell. I realize that this is not a popular thing to say, and in our culture, I could get in trouble for saying it, but it is the truth. If I did not put my faith in Jesus Christ, God would not be unjust in sending me to hell; He would be doing what was absolutely right.

Jesus made very clear in Luke 13 what our sins deserve.[2] On this occasion, some men came to Jesus to get His opinion on what had happened to a group of Galilean worshipers. Apparently, some Galileans had gone to the temple in Jerusalem to worship God, and in the midst of their sacrifices, Pilate brutally executed them. We have a sense of this kind of event since September 11, 2001, when terrorists boarded planes filled with men, women, and children and flew them into the World Trade Center and the Pentagon. Then as now, when something like that happens, it raises questions, and many reporters went to religious leaders to get their perspective on what happened in New York and Washington. In Luke 13, the people went to Jesus.

Luke did not record the explanation they gave for bringing this up, or even whether they asked Jesus a question. He simply recorded that they told Jesus what had happened and what Pilate had done. We do not know exactly how they expected Jesus to respond, but I am sure they did not expect Him to respond the way He did. Jesus completely turned the tables on them. They were thinking about what the tragedy in the temple meant for those Galileans; Jesus wanted them to think about what it meant for them:

> And Jesus said to them, "Do you suppose that these Galileans were greater sinners than all other Galileans because they suffered this fate? . . . Or do you suppose that those eighteen on whom the tower in Siloam fell and killed them [another tragic event in Israel] were worse culprits than all the men who live in Jerusalem? I tell you, no, but unless you repent, you will all likewise perish." (Luke 13:2, 4–5)

Jesus addressed both these questions to a group of people who He assumed believed in judgment. That much is implied in the question itself. They looked at what had happened in the temple and at Siloam and concluded that these people must have died the way they had because they had sinned in an extraordinary way. To them, the only way to explain these tragedies was to see them as God stooping down to judge those individuals for their terrible sins.

In our day, people would look at such disasters and say, "How could that happen to innocent people?" In Jesus' day, they would look at disasters and say, "It must have happened because those people were not innocent." Their fundamental assumption was that those who suffered in unusual ways had to be guilty of greater sins.

We could say that in a sense, those who came and reported this incident to Jesus were ahead of their time because at least they believed in the concept of sin and understood that there is judgment for doing evil. But if they were ahead, they were not far ahead because although they believed in judgment, they had a fundamental misconception about it.

That much is clear because Jesus began His answer in both verses 3 and 5 by saying, "I tell you, no. . . ." In other words, their idea about God's judgment was wrong. The Galileans did not die because they were worse sinners than other Galileans, and those who died when the tower in Siloam fell were not worse culprits than those who lived in Jerusalem. Trying to explain those tragedies in that way was fundamentally wrong.

Many people wish Jesus had stopped there, and the fact is, many people do cut Him off there. They listen to the "I tell you, no," but then ignore the rest of what Jesus had to say and go on to add what they wish He had said. Just this past week, I read of yet another preacher who said that Jesus never spoke of judgment. That is a pretty difficult statement to fathom. It is hard to comprehend how anyone could possibly say something like that with a straight face, especially in light of what Jesus said next in Luke 13.

He did not deny the reality of judgment, but rather their understanding of it. He said that "unless you repent, you will all likewise perish" (13:5). I cannot imagine their faces as they heard Jesus say that. The entire crowd must have gone completely silent.

Question: Does the fact that these people experienced a great tragedy mean that they were more sinful than everyone else?

Answer: No, they were just as sinful as everyone else.

The Galileans did not die because their sin was extraordinarily terrible. Instead, their sin was ordinarily terrible, and if the attitude of those who came and reported this tragedy toward their own sins did not change, they too would perish. In other words, instead of looking at a tragedy like the one that happened in Jerusalem and thinking that our sin must not be all that great because God has not punished us like that, we ought to look at that tragedy, be thankful for God's mercy, and deal with our sin before it is too late, or else God will deal with us just like that.

Jesus flipped the way those men thought about judgment (really, the way most of us tend to think about God's judgment) completely upside down. We look at a tragedy like the one those men reported and think to ourselves, "Those men did not deserve to die like that." And Jesus looks at us and responds, "You have it all wrong. Apart from repentance, you all deserve to die like that. A disaster like this should not surprise you; it should wake you up." John Piper explains:

> What Jesus teaches then is that all of us are extremely sinful. We are so sinful that calamities and disasters should not shock us as though something unwarranted were coming upon innocent human beings. There are no innocent human beings. All have sinned and fall short of the glory of God. There is none righ-

teous, no not one. And what should amaze us is not that some are taken in calamity, but that we are spared and given another day to repent. The really amazing thing in this universe is not that guilty sinners perish, but that God is so slow to anger that you and I can sit here this morning and have one more chance to repent.[3]

When Jesus said, "Unless you repent, you will all likewise perish," it was as if He were saying, "Do not make a mistake about God's patience. Just because God has not punished your sin yet does not mean He won't. God is patient with you so that you have a chance to repent, not because He does not take your sin seriously."

And in fact, we may be sure that this is a promise from Jesus to us as well: if we do not repent of our sin, we will *likewise* perish. When Jesus promised that we would *likewise* perish, He was saying that there is something the unrepentant sinner can learn from what happened in Jerusalem and in Siloam. If we do not repent, there is something similar about the way in which we will perish.

Jesus was not saying that every unrepentant sinner would die at the hands of Pilate in the middle of offering sacrifices at the temple in Jerusalem. We know that because He made the same statement in verse 5, after talking about the tower's falling on those in Siloam. It would be impossible for the unrepentant sinner to die just like the Galileans *and* just like the people in Siloam. So that similarity is out. And Jesus was not merely talking about physical death. After all, He said that if we did repent, we would not perish. And we know that even repentant people die physically.

Jesus was pointing here to a reality beyond the grave. The word *perish* refers to the judgment of God. It is used that way quite often throughout the New Testament. Jesus said in John 3:16, "For God so loved the world . . . that whoever believes in Him shall not perish, but have eternal life." Jesus made a contrast between eternal life and perishing, indicating that perishing refers to eternal death. The apostle Paul explained in Romans 2:12: "For all who have sinned without the Law will also perish without the Law, and all who have sinned under the Law will be judged by the Law. . . ." Paul used the phrases "perish without the Law" and "be judged by the Law" as synonyms. Thus, perishing equals being judged. That makes the best sense in light of what Jesus said about not perishing as a result of repenting. Those who truly repent of their sins will die—they may even die in sudden disasters—but they will not endure the eternal condemnation of God.

Although Jesus was not saying that those who failed to repent would die in exactly the same way as those at Jerusalem and Siloam, He was saying that there was something similar about the way they perished and the way that those who failed to repent would perish. The similarity is simply this: those Galileans did not go to the temple that day thinking they were going to be brutally murdered by Pilate, and those in Siloam did not go to the tower that day thinking it was going to come crashing down on them. Their end came as a terrible surprise to them—and ours will, too, unless we repent.

The point Jesus was making in Luke 13 is that when sudden tragedy strikes, we had better not shake our heads and say, "Tsk, tsk, those people must have been terrible sinners to undergo something like that!" Rather, we ought to view that very tragedy as a reminder that we had better take our sin seriously and repent of it. Otherwise, one day—suddenly and without expecting it—we, too, will face the judgment of God.

Again John Piper explains:

> You see what a horrible end those people came to; they didn't think it was going to happen. Oh, they knew they were going to die someday, but they didn't know what that would mean. The horror of their end took them by surprise. Well, unless you repent, that is the way it is going to be for you. Your end will be far more horrible than you think it is. You will not be ready for it. It will surprise you terribly. In that sense, you will likewise perish.[4]

Jesus was primarily addressing a group of unbelievers who did not take their sin seriously. They did not see their sin for what it was, did not grieve over it and hate it, and had not turned from it to follow Christ. In other words, they had not repented of it. Jesus indicated that their failure to take their sin seriously was linked to a failure to take God's judgment seriously. The reason they did not take God's judgment seriously was that they did not really understand what their sins deserved. Jesus knew that if they were going to take their sin seriously, they had to come face to face with that reality. They had to face the fact that their sin deserved the eternal punishment of God, that there are not certain sins that are deserving of punishment and others that are not.

Sometimes, even as believers, we can become numb to how awful and heinous and serious our seemingly small sins really are. One way we can gain a better understanding of the awfulness of our sin is to look long and hard at the judgment our sin really deserves. We must look at our sins and say what God says about them: that they deserve hell. We must never allow ourselves to doubt that. If we learn to look at sin that way, it will help us to hate it and it will help us to love the One who came to save us from it.

Along with Robert Murray McCheyne, we must remember that "We were over the lake of fire, but it was from this that Jesus saved us; he was in the prison for you and me—he drank every drop out of the cup of God's wrath for you and me; he died the just for the unjust. O beloved, how should we prize, love, and adore Jesus for what he hath done for us. Oh we will never, never know, till safe across Jordan, how our hell has been suffered for us—how our iniquity has been pardoned! But, O beloved! think of hell."[5]

APPLICATION AND DISCUSSION SUGGESTIONS

1. What are some reasons this chapter gives that we do not hate sin even though we know sin wants to destroy us? Can you think of any other reasons that are not mentioned in this chapter?

2. How does our attitude toward sin reveal what we believe about God? For example, what might our attitude about sin reveal about our belief in the omniscience of God? In the holiness of God? In the mercy of God?

3. What is the reason most frequently given in Scripture for people's not taking sin seriously?

4. Summarize what the Bible teaches about hell. What are we tempted to think about hell? Why is hell not unjust?

5. What subtle danger do we as religious people face when thinking about hell?

6. What are some examples of ways in which people divide up sin and sinners in their minds?

7. What needs to happen if you are going to hate sin and be motivated to deal with it?

8. What does Luke 13 teach us about God's judgment and our sin?

9. What can the unrepentant sinner learn from what happened in Jerusalem and Siloam?

10. Why is repentance so important? In light of all that we have seen in the previous chapters, have you repented of your sin?

11. Why does Robert Murray McCheyne say, "O beloved! Think of hell"?

12. How will you be different as a result of what you have learned in this chapter?

HOW TO
PUT SIN
TO DEATH

6

WHAT KILLING YOUR SIN MEANS

In part 1 of this book, we focused on why sin is serious and why we should want to kill it before it kills us. In part 2 we turn to the matter of how to put sin in us to death: we present important issues that are involved in obeying our key texts in Romans 8:13 and Colossians 3:5. We write this section of the book with the biblical conviction that victory over sin is a result of the work of God. "Work out your salvation with fear and trembling; for it is God who is at work in you, both to will and to work for His good pleasure" is the teaching of God's infallible Word (Phil. 2:12–13). Any accomplishment of God's good pleasure is the effect of the work of God. In justification (being declared righteous before God) and sanctification (being made holy in heart and conduct) the flesh profits nothing; man's unaided efforts are useless. Ultimately, God gets all the credit for any spiritual good produced in man or by man.

Yet this does not mean that man's efforts are unimportant. Scripture says that Christians must work out their salvation with fear and trembling and cleanse themselves from all filthiness of the flesh and spirit, perfecting holiness in the fear of God (2 Cor. 7:1; Phil. 2:12). God is always the sanctifier of His people. He is always the One who causes us to triumph, making us more than conquerors through Christ Jesus our Lord. Yet God does not overcome our sin apart from us, but rather by working in us. And it is His working in us that makes our efforts successful. Apart from the help of the triune God, our striving would be losing. With the enablement of the triune God, we are able to conquer temptation and sin.

With that in mind, let's begin to explore the meaning and method of putting sinful desires and deeds to death. We'll begin by asking ourselves some personal questions about sin. Then we'll study the answer to this question: What does it mean to mortify or kill our evil desires and deeds?

Some Personal Questions to Consider

First, think carefully about the following questions and answer them honestly. Do you ever have a problem with sensual appetites, or passions? Do you ever have a problem with impurity? With evil desires? With greed? Do you long for something that you do not have and get a bit jealous because someone else has it? Do you ever have a problem with anger? With wrath? With malice, or ill feelings toward other people? With harboring resentment? With slander? With abusive speech? Do you ever have a problem with deceitfulness, or lying to others?

Surely, if you know anything about yourself and about sin and if you answered the previous questions honestly, you will have to admit that you have a problem in some of the areas mentioned above. And you probably struggle in other areas not mentioned as well. Based on the clear teaching of the Bible, I am sure that not a person in the world can say, "I never had a problem with any of these things, and I don't think I ever will." We all have had problems with many of these things.

The apostle Paul, therefore, was speaking to all of us when he said in Colossians 3:1–9:

> Therefore if you have been raised up with Christ, keep seeking the things above, where Christ is, seated at the right hand of God. Set your mind on the things above, not on the things that are on earth. For you have died and your life is hidden with Christ in God. When Christ, who is our life, is revealed, then you also will be revealed with Him in glory. Therefore consider the members of your earthly body as dead to immorality, impurity, passion, evil desire, and greed, which amounts to idolatry. For it is because of these things that the wrath of God will come upon the sons of disobedience, and in them you also once walked, when you were living in them. But now you also, put them all aside: anger, wrath, malice, slander, and abusive speech from your mouth. Do not lie to one another, since you laid aside the old self with its evil practices. . . .

In verse 5, Paul instructs us to mortify or kill the members of our earthly body. He then lists several specific examples of what we ought to mortify: immorality, impurity, passion (i.e., sensual appetites), evil desire, and greed, which Paul called idolatry. In verse 8, he says that we ought to put off certain things and then specified some of those things: anger, wrath, malice, slander, and abusive speech. In verse 9, he continues in the same manner when he instructs us to put off lying to one another, considering that we have put off the old man with his deeds.

What Putting Sin to Death Does Not Mean

What does Paul mean when he commands us to mortify or kill the members of our earthly bodies? First, let's consider what he does *not* mean. He does not mean that we are to eradicate sin or to eradicate our evil desires to the extent that they will never trouble us again. That is impossible in this life, though there are some who would have us believe that it's possible. They say that if we do thus and such, if we apply a certain formula, if we say the right prayers and go to the right places and do the right things, we can have our sin nature completely removed—eradicated forever. They say that we can attain sinless perfection. Some have actually said that if we live by the right formula, we can be as spotless and sinless as Jesus. They tell us that we can arrive at the place where we will never again have to get down on our knees and ask God for forgiveness. The prayer of the publican will be unnecessary for us—we will never have to say, "God, have mercy on me, a sinner."

I submit to you, however, that this view is contrary both to experience and to Scripture. The greatest saints in the history of the church have been those who have recognized their sinfulness more and more the longer they have lived. The greatest Christians have constantly cried out to God for forgiveness. The greatest saints have always been people who have recognized that they were great sinners.

Scripture does not teach sinless perfection here on this earth. It was the apostle Paul who said in Philippians 3:12–14, "Not that I have already obtained it or have already become perfect, but I press on so that I may lay hold of that for which also I was laid hold of by Christ Jesus. Brethren, I do not regard myself as having laid hold of it yet; but one thing I do: forgetting what lies behind and reaching forward to what lies ahead, I press on toward the goal for the prize of the upward call of God in Christ Jesus." When Paul made this statement, he was not a young Christian, but rather a Christian of almost thirty years. He was in prison at the time and knew that he might be put to death. And yet this Paul, who had lived a life that was as close to the Lord as it is possible for a man to live, declared that he was not perfect.

Again in 1 Timothy 1:15, Paul wrote, "It is a trustworthy statement, deserving full acceptance, that Christ Jesus came into the world to save sinners, among whom I am foremost of all." Notice that he did not say "among whom I *was* foremost of all."

The apostle John also said, "If we say that we have no sin, we are deceiving ourselves and the truth is not in us. If we confess our sins, He is faithful and righteous to forgive us our sins and to cleanse us from all unrighteousness. If we say that we have not sinned, we make Him a liar and His word is not in us" (1 John 1:8–10). John declared that if we claim to have no sin, we are not kidding anyone but ourselves. We are deceiving ourselves, and the truth is not in us. And so the Bible makes it clear that until the day we die, we will have a problem with evil desires—with our old sinful nature.

So when the apostle Paul said to "consider the members of your earthly body as dead" in Colossians 3:5, he was not talking about sinless perfection. He was not talking about the complete eradication of all our evil desires. What, then, did he mean? I believe that he meant at least three things.

What Putting Sin to Death Means

First, Paul meant that we should deprive our evil desires of their strength and of their power. The Amplified Bible's version of the New Testament tells us that the Greek word translated "mortify" can also be translated "kill (deaden, deprive of power)."

Perhaps someone reading this book has, in the past, had a great problem in some area of life. Perhaps it was a problem with pride. Or a problem with anger. Or a problem with a sharp tongue, or evil thoughts, or loose living. Perhaps it was very easy to break the commandment "Thou shalt not commit adultery" in the person's mind, if not in actual behavior. Today the person may still have that same problem, but perhaps it is not as great as it once was because it has been robbed of its power. If it were allowed to, it could become just as great as before, but it has been deprived or robbed of its power.

One man told me that he used to have a tremendous problem with his temper. He would fly into a rage and begin to use his fists. Today he would admit that if he were not careful, he would still have that same problem. That old evil desire is there, but it has been robbed, it has been deprived, of its power, and now it is largely under control. The same thing is true with other people in reference to pride, alcohol, or loose living. They don't have the problems with these things that they once had. This is in part what Paul is talking about when he says to consider evil desires as dead. We should do everything we can to rob these evil desires of their power.

Second, when the apostle Paul said that we are to consider the members of our earthly body as dead to sin, he meant that we should fight against those evil desires. In at least thirty different passages of Scripture, Paul said that we ought to fight, wrestle, and strive against evil desires. In other words, we ought to be at war with them. For example, Ephesians 6:10–13 says:

> Finally, be strong in the Lord and in the strength of His might. Put on the full armor of God, so that you will be able to stand firm against the schemes of the devil. For our struggle is not against flesh and blood, but against the rulers, against the powers, against the world forces of this darkness, against the spiritual forces of wickedness in the heavenly places. Therefore, take up the full armor of God, so that you will be able to resist in the evil day, and having done everything, to stand firm.

Likewise, 1 Timothy 6:12 challenges us, "Fight the good fight of faith; take hold of the eternal life to which you were called. . . ." Paul was reminding us that life is a battle.

Indeed, the Christian life is a fight. It is the good fight of faith whereby we lay hold of eternal life. If anyone thinks that the Christian life is easy, he knows very little about it. In fact, it is doubtful that he is a Christian at all, because the Christian life from its conception to its consummation is a battle. It is a life-and-death struggle with the world, the flesh, and the devil. In 2 Timothy 2:3–5, Paul encouraged us, "Suffer hardship with me, as a good soldier of Christ Jesus. No soldier in active service entangles himself in the affairs of everyday life, so that he may please the one who enlisted him as a soldier. Also if anyone competes as an athlete, he does not win the prize unless he competes according to the rules."

First Corinthians 16:13 calls out, "Be on the alert, stand firm in the faith, act like men, be strong." These are military terms. The Christian is to fight, he is to battle, he is to wrestle, he is to struggle against the evil desires that lurk within, which would lead him into sin. This is part of what it means to consider ourselves dead to evil desires.

Third, to consider the members of our earthly body as dead to sin means to overcome particular evil desires when they arise in our lives. It means to put the evil desire to death and lay it in the grave. In 1 Peter 2:11, Peter said, "Beloved, I urge you as aliens and strangers to abstain from fleshly lusts which wage war against the soul." When I, by the grace of God, am made able to abstain from a fleshly lust that arises and wages war against my soul, I have killed that particular fleshly lust.

In Colossians 3:8, Paul wrote, "But now you also, put them all aside: anger, wrath, malice, slander, and abusive speech from your mouth." When the temptation comes for me to sin—to lose my temper, to harbor bitterness in my heart toward another person, or to use abusive talk about another person—and I, by the grace of God, am able to overcome it, in that instance I have killed that evil desire. To consider ourselves as dead to these evil desires, therefore, means to overcome them as they come to tempt us.

In concluding this chapter on what it means to put sinful desires and deeds to death, I would like to borrow a section from Jerry Bridges's book *The Gospel for Real Life*. I believe this section will help us to understand the basis, the importance, and the meaning of the issue we have been discussing. Bridges writes:

We [as believers] have died not only to sin's guilt, but also to its reigning power in our lives. . . . As an analogy to help us understand, the will to live is an active principle within us. With few exceptions the principle always asserts itself when we are faced with a life-threatening situation. We instinctively fight to save our lives.

Now, although sin as an active principle is still with us, it can no longer reign supreme in our lives. We are united to Christ, and His Holy Spirit has come to reside in us. We have been delivered from the power of Satan and given a new heart (see Ezekiel 36:26; Acts 26:18). However, as believers we do experience the tension Paul describes in Galatians 5:17. . . .

George Smeaton described this tension in this way: there is an internal conflict between the flesh and spirit—between an old nature and new nature. And the strange thing is, that in this conflict the power and faculties of the Christian seem to be occupied at one time by one, and at another time by another. The same intellect, will, and affections come under different influences, like two conflicting armies occupying the same ground, and in turn driven from the field.

Another way of describing this tension between the sinful nature and the Spirit is to liken it to a tug of war. With two opposing teams pulling on the rope, its direction of movement often goes back and forth until one team eventually prevails. This is the way it will be with us until the Holy Spirit prevails.

We must acknowledge this tension if we are to make progress in the Christian life. Indwelling sin is like a disease that we can't begin to deal with until we acknowledge its presence. But in the case of sin, though it still resides in us, it no longer has dominion over us. As Paul said, "For sin shall not be your master, because you are not under law, but under grace" (Romans 6:14).

Therefore, because we have the assurance that sin shall not be our master, we are not to let it reign in our mortal bodies so that we obey its evil desires (Romans 6:12). Rather we are, by the enabling power of the Spirit, to put to death the misdeeds of the body (Romans 8:13), and to abstain from sinful desires, which war against our souls (1 Peter 2:11). Indeed, we are called to an active, vigorous warfare against the principle of sin that remains in us.[1]

In this quotation, Bridges uses some analogies to help us understand what it means to put evil desires and deeds to death. First, he uses the analogy from George Smeaton about two conflicting armies competing for the same territory. The sin principle within us still attempts to take over the whole territory of our lives, and we must actively fight against it to overcome it. The second analogy Bridges uses is that of a tug-of-war. Bridges suggests that even though we may be real Christians, there remains in us a sin principle that will tug at us to fulfill its desires in doing what is sinful. Third, Bridges uses the idea of a disease. He compares this remaining sin principle to a disease that is in us, and indicates that we cannot and will not be able to successfully deal with this disease until we recognize its presence and take appropriate measures to deal with it.

The sin principle to which Bridges refers is what theologians such as John Owen call "indwelling sin," which is a holdover from our pre-Christian life, from the nature we inherited from Adam. In our union with Christ, its power has been demolished, but not its entire presence and influence. So we can and we must fight it. By the power of the Holy Spirit, using the procedures laid out in God's Word, we can mortify (kill) its power at the times when we are tempted to obey its evil desires and perform its evil deeds.

In this passage, Bridges also rightly indicates that this struggle, or what he calls tension, will go on throughout our entire lives. In other words, the war has been won through the death and resurrection of Christ and our union with Him, but there will still be battles with indwelling sin that we must fight as long as we are in this world. Because of our union with Christ and the indwelling presence of the powerful Holy Spirit, we do not have to lose the battles—sin will no more have dominion over us. Nevertheless, though the war has been won and victory over the individual battles is possible, we cannot avoid the necessity of regularly and frequently fighting those battles. The necessity of putting evil desires and deeds to death will require our constant attention.

APPLICATION AND DISCUSSION SUGGESTIONS

1. Write out in full on 3x5 cards Romans 8:13 and Colossians 3:5.

2. Make it a practice to repeat and spend some time meditating on these texts in the morning, at noon, and in the evening.

3. Why is the failure to put the deeds of the body to death such a serious matter? Give biblical support for your answer.

4. What three things mentioned in this chapter are involved in doing what the apostle Paul is commanding us to do?

5. According to this chapter, what *wasn't* the apostle Paul referring to when he told us to kill or mortify sin?

6. What biblical evidence is there to support what this chapter presents as the meaning of putting sin to death?

7. Do you have any other ideas about what the apostle Paul meant when he commanded us to "put the deeds of the body to death" (Rom. 8:13) or to "put that which is earthly in us to death" (Col. 3:5)? (Suggestion: You might want to check some good commentaries or read volume 6 of *The Works of John Owen*.)

8. Summarize the teaching of each of the following texts and explain how they relate to Paul's commands in Romans 8:13 and Colossians 3:5: 1 Corinthians 16:13–14; Philippians 3:12–14; Colossians 3:1–4; 2 Timothy 2:3–4; 1 Peter 2:11.

9. What three analogies does Jerry Bridges use to illustrate the tension of the Christian life?

10. What is the meaning and significance of each of these analogies for the Christian life?

11. Do you regularly carry out the sin-killing practices described in this chapter? Try to think of specific examples of times when you did.

12. What practical applications for your Christian life will you make from this chapter?

7

YOU CAN KILL YOUR
SIN BECAUSE . . .

If we are children of God, the Holy Spirit has a vital ministry in our lives. Everything we do as a child of God is dependent on the Holy Spirit. Without Him, we can do nothing. " 'Not by might nor by power, but by My Spirit,' says the LORD of Hosts" (Zech. 4:6). And yet the Bible says that we can grieve the Holy Spirit so that He is quenched and no longer ministers to us as He once did (Eph. 4:30; 1 Thess. 5:19).

How do we grieve the Holy Spirit? Ephesians 4:25–32 indicates that we grieve Him by allowing sin to remain unmortified in our lives. We grieve the Holy Spirit by lying instead of speaking the truth, by slothfulness instead of diligence, by stealing instead of sharing, by unwholesome and abusive speech instead of profitable and gracious speech. The Spirit of God is the Holy Spirit, and we will know little of His gracious influence if we coddle sin rather than put it to death.

You Can't Do It by Yourself, and You Don't Need To

As mentioned in previous chapters, even though we are Christians, we are involved in a battle—a battle with "the lusts of the flesh," a battle that is too much for us, a battle in which we need divine assistance if we are going to win. Paul knew this well, and he frequently wrote about the solution to the problem. To win this battle, he told the Galatians, we must "walk by the Spirit." He continued by saying that if we would walk by the Spirit, we "will not carry out the desire of the flesh" (Gal. 5:16). To the Roman Christians, he said:

> For the law of the Spirit of life in Christ Jesus has set you free from the law [i.e., controlling power] of sin and of death. . . . But if the Spirit of Him who raised Jesus from the dead dwells in you, He who raised Christ Jesus from the dead will also give life to your mortal bodies through His Spirit who dwells in you. So then, brethren, we are under obligation, not to the flesh, to live according to the flesh—for if you are living according to the flesh, you must die; but if by the Spirit you are putting to death the deeds of the body, you will live. (Rom. 8:2, 11–13)

In these passages, Paul was saying that the flesh (or our old nature) will still harass us, but the good news is that we are not under obligation to the flesh. No longer are we obliged to be controlled by the flesh. We can overcome; we can win. We can win the battle because the Spirit of God lives in us, and through His power we can put to death the desires and deeds of the flesh. In no uncertain terms, Paul indicated that we must put to death the deeds of the flesh, but more than that, he asserted that we can put them to death by the Spirit. The Holy Spirit is our main source of power. If we avail ourselves of His ministry and walk in the Spirit, we will win. Conversely, these passages indicate that we will lose this battle if we fail to walk in the Spirit. According to Paul, there is no alternative. It is an either/or proposition: either walk by the Spirit and overcome, or walk in the flesh and lose.[1]

In volume 3 of his outstanding series on important issues in the Christian life, John Owen put it this way:

> We are not able of ourselves, without the especial aid, assistance of the Spirit of God, in any measure or degree to free ourselves from this pollution. It is true it is frequently prescribed upon us as our duty . . . , but to suppose that . . . we have the power of ourselves to do this, is to make the cross of Christ of none effect. . . . Of ourselves, therefore, we are not able, by any endeavors of our own, nor ways of finding out, to cleanse ourselves from the defilement of sin. . . . Until His Spirit is formed in us . . . we cannot perform any one act that is spiritually good, nor any one act of vital obedience.[2]

To put sin to death in keeping with the truth of Romans 8:13 and Galatians 5:16, we must walk in the Spirit. Unless we do it by the Spirit, killing the desires and deeds of the flesh is impossible. Without the enablement of the Spirit, it simply will not get done. But then the question arises: What does it mean to walk in the Spirit? To answer that question, I want to borrow, in an abbreviated form, from chapter 10 of our book *God's Solutions to Life's Problems*, where an expansive answer is given. In that chapter, we state that walking in the Spirit:

1. Involves relying completely on the Spirit for every aspect of the Christian life.
2. Means living in the consciousness of His personal presence in us and with us.
3. Involves memorizing, meditating on, believing, and living God's Word because the Bible is the Spirit's book.
4. Means that you will think much about Jesus because the Holy Spirit has come to glorify Christ (John 16:14).
5. Involves trusting the credibility of the Holy Spirit, that He will do what He has said He will do (John 16:8–9; Acts 1:8; Rom. 8:2–4; 8:26; 1 Cor. 2:14–16; 6:11; 2 Cor. 3:18; 13:14; Gal. 5:22–23; Eph. 3:16–18; 4:30; 2 Tim. 1:7).
6. Means that you will be willing to do what the Spirit tells you to do in His Word. The believer who is walking in the Spirit must be willing to go where the Holy Spirit guides and leads him to go, and do what the Holy Spirit guides and leads him to do in His Word. He seeks to obey the Holy Spirit, and he trusts that the Spirit of God will give him the power to carry out the Spirit's directions.
7. Means walking thought by thought, decision by decision, act by act under the Spirit's control.[3]

The Death of Christ and Its Relationship to Killing Our Sin

To put sin to death, we should also reflect often on the meaning and purpose of Christ's death. First Peter 2:24 explains the purpose of Christ's death in this way: "He Himself bore our sins in His body on the cross, so that we might die to sin and live to righteousness. . . ." In similar fashion, Titus 2:14 declares that Christ "gave Himself for us to redeem us from every lawless deed, and to purify for Himself a people for His own possession, zealous for good deeds." In this verse, Paul was teaching that through the death of Jesus Christ on our behalf, we who have come to Christ have been set free (redeemed) from the penalty and power of our sin. The word *redeem* reminds us that we were in bondage to lawlessness. Violating and breaking God's law was a lifestyle for us. But Christ came to redeem us from this bondage. Now, being in Christ, we do not have to continue to violate God's law. We can, through the redemption of Jesus Christ, now walk in newness of life and live a life of holiness and obedience.

Still further, Scripture asserts that through the death of Jesus Christ we have been purified, cleansed, made pure. God has cleaned us up on the inside. Scripture teaches us that before we came to Jesus Christ, our hearts were desperately wicked and deceitful above all things (Jer. 17:9), incapable of doing anything that was good or righteous in the sight of God (Mark 7:21; Rom. 3:10–18).

In our book *God's Solutions to Life's Problems*, we write that Paul's words in Titus 2:14

"bring to mind the picture of a man standing on the auction block at an ancient slave market. Stolen from or sold by his parents at an early age, he has lived years in bondage to a cruel master. And now he stands there on the auction block to be sold like an animal. Someone in the crowd cries out, 'I'll take him for a hundred denarii.' The slave doesn't even lift his head to see who bought him because he knows nothing is going to change. He's just going from one master to another. He's still looking down when his new owner comes up to him and gently says to him, 'You are free. You have been redeemed. I paid the price and you are free.' If this were to occur, the freed slave would have been ecstatic with joy. . . . He would have loved his redeemer. . . . That's what Paul says Christ has done for us. We were slaves to sin and Satan, but Christ has ransomed us. He has paid the price to set us free from our bondage to living a life characterized by disobedience to God's law. To put sin to death requires an understanding of this aspect of what Christ's sacrifice on the cross really accomplished for us."[4]

Scripture teaches that before we became Christians, our minds and consciences were defiled and that we were alienated from and hostile in our minds to God (Rom. 8:7; Col. 1:21–23). We not only had a problem with guilt, possessing a bad record, but also had the problem of a dirty, defiled, and corrupt heart—every imagination of our hearts was only evil continually (Gen. 8:21; Eccl. 9:3). Scripture, however, declares that through the work of Jesus Christ on the cross on our behalf, God has not only dealt with the problem of our bad record (our guilt), but also dealt with the problem of our bad heart (our inner corruption). He has purified us unto Himself as a people for His own possession. We now belong to Him, and by His grace, He enables us to put to death the desires and deeds of the flesh and to perform good works that bring glory to Him. As Hebrews 9:14 states, "the blood of Christ, who . . . offered Himself without blemish to God, cleanse[s] your conscience . . . to serve the living God." God, through Christ, cleans us up. He purifies us on the inside, making it possible for us to say "no" to "ungodliness and worldly desires and to live sensibly, righteously and godly in the present age" (Titus 2:12).

In commenting on this aspect of what Christ has done for us, our book *God's Solutions to Life's Problems* reminds us of Paul's words in Romans 7:18 that "nothing good dwells in me." In other words, Paul knew that the corruption of sin goes far beyond our actions; it goes to our very hearts. We are defiled by what is already in us, not by what happens around us. Evil propensities come from within because we come into this world with corrupt and defiled hearts (Mark 7:21–23). We do evil things because we are evil, unclean, and unpurified. We do what we do because we are what we are—corrupt and defiled within (Eph. 2:3). Our evil actions are the overflow of our pre-purified hearts.

Before Christ purifies us, we are like a sponge from which ink flows when squeezed. The ink comes out because there is ink within, not simply because the sponge is squeezed. So it is with us. The ungodly actions, thoughts, words, affections, and desires come out of us because of the unpurified condition of our hearts.

What do we need so that our actions, reactions, thoughts, words, affections, and desires will be God-honoring and pleasing? We need to be purged and cleansed from our internal filthiness. How is this accomplished? We need a Savior who will clean us up on the inside, and we have that in Jesus Christ, who gave Himself for us so that we might be purified for Himself as a people for His own possession. And then, having been purified, we are therefore able to do works that are good in His sight (Titus 2:14).[5]

Continually remembering, reflecting on, and believing that Titus 2:14 is accurately describing what Christ's death accomplished for us is an essential factor in the mortification of sin in our Christian life. This great truth makes victory over sin a possibility in our daily lives.

UNDERSTANDING HOW OUR SIN REFLECTS ON CHRIST

To put sin to death, we should also consider how sin reflects on the Lord Jesus Christ. If we are Christians and indulge in sin, how does this reflect on our Lord? The Bible says that "you shall call His name Jesus, for He will save His people from their sins" (Matt. 1:21). Again, Titus 2:14 says that Christ "gave Himself for us to redeem us from every lawless deed, and to purify for Himself a people for His own possession, zealous for good deeds." And Ephesians 5:25–26 teaches that "Christ also loved the church and gave Himself up for her, so that He might sanctify her, having cleansed her by the washing of water with the word."

A workman is known by his work. We look at a man's paint job and get an idea of the man himself: he is either sloppy or neat. We look at a chair that someone has made and get an idea of what kind of carpenter he is. People look at us and, whether we like it or not, they get an idea of Jesus Christ. In other words, they associate Christ with what they see in us.

In 2 Samuel 12:13–14 we read, "And Nathan said to David, 'The LORD also has taken away your sin; you shall not die. However, because by this deed you have given occasion to the enemies of the LORD to blaspheme, the child also that is born to you shall surely die." God will forgive us of our sins if we are truly believers, but that does not erase or change the fact that our open sin has given the enemies of Jesus Christ an opportunity to say, "Is that all that Jesus Christ can do?"

APPLICATION AND DISCUSSION SUGGESTIONS

1. List the things mentioned in this chapter that we should do to help us put Romans 8:13 and Colossians 3:5–9 into practice in our lives.

2. List the Scriptures that support the importance of doing the things mentioned in this chapter if we want to actually fulfill the commands of Romans 8:13 and Colossians 3:9.

3. What does it mean to grieve the Holy Spirit?

4. How do we grieve the Holy Spirit?

5. Why is grieving the Holy Spirit a serious matter for Christians?

6. What does the word *redeem* (used in Titus 2:14) suggest about our condition and what Christ does for believers?

7. What does the word *purify* (Titus 2:14) suggest about our condition and what Christ does for believers?

8. How can practicing the things suggested in this chapter help you to fulfill the commands of Romans 8:13 and Colossians 3:5–9?

9. Select two verses mentioned in this chapter, write them out in full on 3x5 cards, and work on memorizing them.

10. Make it a practice to repeat and spend some time meditating on these texts in the morning, at noon, and in the evening. Seek to put them into practice when you are confronted by temptations to sin.

11. Keep a record of what these temptations were, how and when they occurred, and how and why you responded as you did.

12. Do you regularly carry out the sin-killing practices described in this chapter? Try to think of specific examples of times you did. Be ready to share them with your discussion group or counselor.

13. What practical applications will you make to your life after reading this chapter?

8

REMEMBER,
YOU DON'T SIN ALONE

We closed the previous chapter by explaining that the consideration of how and why our sin reflects badly on Jesus Christ is an important part of putting sin to death in our lives. The point is that if we truly understand the great love of Christ that motivated Him to lay down His life for us (2 Cor. 5:14–15), this fact ought to motivate us to put sin to death. If we know His love for us and love Him in return, how can we not be motivated to hate sin and want to kill it in our daily lives (1 John 4:9–11, 19)?

THE RIPPLE EFFECT OF OUR SIN

I would like to begin this chapter by further considering the destructive effects of our sin, which not only reflects poorly on Christ, but affects other people as well. We need to remember that when we go down, we usually drag someone else with us. Our sin has a ripple effect; it spreads out and affects those around us. We sow and others reap along with us—or perhaps I should say because of us. When Eve disobeyed God and ate of the forbidden fruit (Gen. 2:15–17), it wasn't long before Adam was also disobeying and eating (Gen. 3:6). Eve's sin affected her husband—and beyond that, their sin had a ripple effect on their children. Their son Cain would have never become angry as he did, or lied to God, or killed his brother, apart from the sin of his father and mother. In fact, the ripple effect—or consequences—of their sin went far beyond even that. Romans 5:12 indicates that all the sin committed by any of the descendants of Adam and Eve (including you and me) can be traced back to Adam and Eve's sin in Genesis 3.

Numerous biblical texts and examples teach us that no one sins alone and no one experiences the consequences of his sins without affecting others. One such example is found in 1 Corinthians 5:1–12. In this passage, Paul wrote that he had received a report about a young fellow in the church who was openly and continually practicing immorality. He had also been informed that the church in which that man was involved was allowing this to continue without doing anything about it. Having heard that, Paul confronted the Corinthians for their neglect in no uncertain terms. Indeed, he used some of the strongest words of challenge and rebuke found in all the Pauline epistles. From what he wrote, it is evident that he was horrified and alarmed at their indolence. He accused them of being arrogant and said that they should have mourned for the sin of this young man. Then Paul gave them some very specific directions: "The one who [has] done this deed [should] be removed from your midst. For I . . . , though absent in body but present in spirit, have already judged him who has so committed this, as though I were present. In the name of our Lord Jesus, when you are assembled, . . . deliver such a one to Satan for the destruction of his flesh, so that his spirit may be saved in the day of the Lord Jesus" (5:2–5).

Finally, having chastised and instructed the Corinthians, he proceeded to explain why it was so important for them to do something about this person's flagrant sin rather than overlook it. The reason is found in these words: "Do you not know that a little leaven leavens the whole lump of dough? Clean out the old leaven so that you may be a new lump . . ." (5:6–7). "Leaven" in this passage refers to the sin that is being practiced and ignored. Paul's reasoning was that just as a little leaven in a batch of dough will affect the whole loaf, so allowing flagrant and unrepented sin to continue will not only affect the man himself, but also affect the whole church. In other words, personal sin not only affects the person who is sinning, but also affects others with whom he is associated.

Another example of this same phenomenon is found in Hebrews 12:12–13: "Therefore, strengthen the hands that are weak and the knees that are feeble, and make straight paths for your feet, so that the limb which is lame may not be put out of joint, but rather be healed." In this text, the writer was using weak hands and feeble knees as metaphors for spiritual experiences. The *New Testament Commentary* suggests that in this passage, the author was functioning as a coach by using some phrases that were familiar to his readers to motivate them to enthusiastic and continuing action (Job 4:3–4; Prov. 4:26;

Isa. 35:3–4).[1] What is going on here is that the Christian life is being pictured as a race (Heb. 12:1), a race that is not yet finished, a race in which some of the athletes are becoming tired and their hands and knees are weak.

What do these weary and fatigued Christians need at this point so that they will run with endurance the race that is set before them? How will the writer motivate them to renew their enthusiasm, to lift up their weak hands and strengthen their feeble knees? He does so by reminding them that if they falter, others will be affected by their faltering. He reminds them that there are other runners who are handicapped—they are lame and will be hindered by another runner's faltering. In other words, he was challenging them to keep in mind that what they do will have a positive or negative influence on others.

Continuing on in the same passage, the Bible says, "Pursue peace with all men, and the sanctification without which no one will see the Lord. See to it that no one comes short of the grace of God; that no root of bitterness springing up causes trouble, and by it many be defiled" (12:14–15). "Watch out!" the writer warned them. "Don't let any root of bitterness spring up in you because if it does, not only is it going to affect you, it is going to affect others. Because of your bitterness, many others are going to be defiled."

This fact ought to put us on our knees before Almighty God, who visits the iniquities of the fathers upon the third and fourth generations (Ex. 34:7). Mothers should realize that their loose tongues—their constant complaining about the people of God or the church—may be the very instrument that the devil uses in turning their children away from Jesus Christ and the church. Fathers should realize that when they constantly yield to evil desires, their children are observing them. When children know that their fathers claim to be Christians, but they see them indulging in sin, they say, "If that is what a Christian is, I don't want to be like my dad."

To put sin to death, therefore, we must meditate often on the dangerous effects of sin. Let us not be guilty of making the same mistake as the young man in Proverbs 7, who walked into sin unaware. Scripture says that this man did not know that yielding to sin was serious. He never gave what he was doing a second thought. Scripture says that he lacked sense. He thought he could get away with it without unpleasant consequences. He failed to put his evil desires and deeds to death and therefore went as an ox to the slaughter and as a bird into a snare. In keeping with the truth of 1 Corinthians 10:11, what we find in this story is included for our learning so that we would avoid making the mistake the young man made. This story shouts at us the message that if we would overcome, if we would have victory over sin, we must load our consciences, our minds, and our hearts with the heinousness and peril of sin. We must come to the Word of God and get God's point of view on sin.

WATCH OUT!

The words of our Lord Jesus Christ in Matthew 26:41 point to another important principle involved in killing sin in us. Here Jesus said, "Keep watching and praying that you may not enter into temptation; the spirit is willing, but the flesh is weak." The word translated *watching* in this passage literally means that we should "be on our guard." It means to keep alert or to stay awake. The fact that the verb is in the active voice, imperative mood, present tense conveys essential information about gaining victory over sin. The active voice means that it is something we must *personally* do (it will not be done for us). The imperative mood indicates that it is something we must *willfully* do (it will not just automatically happen; we cannot be passive). The present tense teaches us that it is something we must *constantly* do (there will never come a time in our lives in this world when what Jesus is commanding us to do will be unnecessary; we must constantly be watching or we will be defeated).

The same Greek word for *watching* is used in Acts 20:28–31, where Paul told the Ephesian elders that grievous wolves would enter in among them, not sparing the flock, "and from among your own selves men will arise, speaking perverse things, to draw away the disciples after them. Therefore be on the alert, remembering that night and day for a period of three years I did not cease to admonish each one with tears" (vv. 30–31). Paul assured the Ephesian elders that men would come into their church from the outside and also rise up from within to seek to draw away disciples after themselves, teaching error instead of the truth of God's Word. Because this was surely going to happen, Paul urged the elders to watch, stay alert, look out for these false teachers, and be ready to defend the church against them.

Peter sounded out the same note in 1 Peter 5:8: "Be of sober spirit, be on the alert. Your adversary, the devil, prowls around like a roaring lion, seeking someone to devour." Peter warned us of the subtlety and cruelty of the devil, who is constantly active, trying to destroy us. Therefore, we must be sober and vigilant or we will most certainly be destroyed.

According to the Bible, doing what Romans 8:13 and Colossians 3:5 command will require watching, but what does it mean to watch? The answer is straightforward: watching is the very opposite of going to sleep; a man who is asleep is certainly not watching.

There are times when sleep is a blessing. Take, for example, a man who has many problems. He has countless bills, his creditors are hounding him for money, and he lives with a nagging wife. To add to this, his children are sick. He is not doing too well in his work, and he does not know how long he will have his job. His car breaks down and the mechanic tells him that fixing it will be expensive. He comes home at night beaten and exhausted. He goes to bed and, out of sheer exhaustion, goes to sleep. While he is asleep, he loses contact with reality. He has some pleasant dreams, and when he wakes up in the morning, he is somewhat refreshed. He feels much better; he is ready to face his problems. For this man, sleep has been a blessing.

But there are times when sleep is a curse. If a man who is driving down the highway becomes drowsy, this is not a blessing. As he sees the oncoming lights and hears the hum of the motor, his head begins to nod. He tries to fight sleep. He rolls down the window, sticks his head out, and drives that way for a while, hoping that the air will wake him up. He turns on the radio and increases the volume, thinking that the noise will help to keep him awake. He begins to talk to himself and slap himself on the face to arouse himself. But in spite of all his efforts, his head still nods. Finally, his head goes down for just a few seconds. His arms relax, the steering wheel turns, and he veers into the path of an oncoming car. There is a crash, and he enters eternity. For that man, sleep was not a blessing; it was a curse.

In many places, the Bible refers to a condition of spiritual drowsiness or spiritual sleep. When it does, this condition is always described as perilous or dangerous. Again and again in the Word of God, people who are spiritually drowsy are called on to awaken. Scripture says: "Become sober-minded as you ought, and stop sinning; for some have no knowledge of God. I speak this to your shame" (1 Cor. 15:34). "Go to the ant, O sluggard, observe her ways and be wise, which, having no chief, office or ruler, prepares her food in the summer and gathers her provision in the harvest. How long will you lie down, O sluggard? When will you arise from your sleep? 'A little sleep, a little slumber, a little folding of the hands to rest'—your poverty will come in like a vagabond and your need like an armed man" (Prov. 6:6–11).

In the physical realm, there are many who cannot be blamed for their poverty because they are sick, are weak, or do not have advantageous opportunities. But when a man is a sluggard and spends too much time in bed, that man becomes poor of his own doing. Because of his slothfulness, he experiences poverty just as truly as if a robber had broken into his house and stolen all his goods, or just as though a strong, armed man had bound him and kept him from working.

Tragically, many are spiritually poor because they are spiritually lazy or even sleeping. Such a "professing Christian" never amounts to anything. So God says, "Wake up!" In Luke 21:34, Jesus warned, "Be on guard, so that your hearts will not be weighted down with dissipation and drunkenness and the worries of life. . . ." Jesus is urging us to watch against all occasions or circumstances that might stir up sin in our hearts. Our evil desires and inclinations may be compared to a fire that has died down. As long as the ashes are left alone, the fire will do no damage. But if someone stirs up the dying embers, that fire may become a raging inferno.

Our evil desires may also be compared to sediment at the bottom of a pool. As long as the sediment remains on the bottom, the water is clear. But if someone stirs up the sediment, the whole pool becomes cloudy and dirty. At times the fire of our evil desires burns low, but then some circumstance arises and the fire blazes furiously. Likewise, at times the sediment of our wicked inclinations seems to settle, but then some person or event provides the means by which they are stirred up again.

Some years ago, a man was having some physical problems. He had a burning sensation in the top of his stomach. For a time he ignored it, but it was so persistent and annoying that he finally went to a doctor. After examining him, the doctor said, "You look pretty healthy. I don't see anything wrong with you. You are probably working too hard. Slow down just a bit, and I think you will be all right." The man tried to follow the doctor's advice, but the problem continued. So he contacted his doctor again, and the doctor said, "You had better have some X-rays taken. Maybe you have a problem with your gallbladder." When the gallbladder tests came back negative, the doctor said, "Maybe you have an ulcer." More X-rays were taken—also negative. "Well," said the doctor, "you must have an over-acid condition, so I will put you on a diet. If you eat the right foods, you will be fine."

The doctor was right. The man discovered that when he stayed on his diet, the burning sensation in his stomach disappeared. He also discovered that when he went off his diet, the burning sensation reappeared. This man overcame his physical problem by watching his diet. Likewise, Jesus said that if we are to overcome our evil desires, we must be on our guard against those things that stir them up.

Scripture says, "For the lips of an adulteress drip honey and smoother than oil is her speech; but in the end she is bitter as wormwood, sharp as a two-edged sword. Her feet go down to death, her steps take hold of Sheol. She does not ponder the path of life; her ways are unstable, she does not know it. Now then, my sons, listen to me and do not depart from the words of my mouth. Keep your way far from her and do not go near the door of her house" (Prov. 5:3–8). Here we have the sound advice of a father to his son, whom he instructed, "If you want to overcome sin, stay away from the person or circumstances that especially appeal to your evil desires."

Again, in another passage, this same father pleaded with his son, "My son, if sinners entice you, do not consent. . . . My son, do not walk in the way with them. Keep your feet from their path" (Prov. 1:10, 15). He urged his son, "If sinners entice you, if they tempt you, stay away from them! Do not even associate with them. Avoid those occasions or circumstances that have a tendency to stir up your evil desires."

Many years ago, in horse-and-buggy days, a man advertised for a coach driver. His offer included a big salary and many benefits. He had numerous applicants for the position. After studying the applications, he eliminated all but four men. Then he invited each of those four for an interview. One by one they were brought in and asked the same question: "We are out in the countryside, traveling on a narrow road, and there is a mountain on one side and a deep, sharp cliff on the other. How close could you drive to the cliff and not go over?" Three of the men stated that they could come within a foot of the cliff and still not go over. The fourth man said, "I would stay as far away from the cliff as I could." That man got the job.

Many professing Christians seem to have this attitude: "How close can I come to sin without actually sinning?" Or: "How much sin can I commit and still be a Christian?" This is a wrong attitude. We are to stay as far away from sin as possible. Jesus said, "If your hand causes you to stumble, cut it off; . . . if your foot causes you to stumble, cut it off; . . . if your eye causes you to stumble, throw it out; it is better for you to enter the kingdom of God with one eye, than, having two eyes, to be cast into hell" (Mark 9:43–47).

Of course, Jesus did not mean that we should literally cut off a hand or foot or pluck out an eye if they cause us problems. Jesus was saying that if something causes us to stumble, if something stirs up our evil desires and leads us into sin, it must be put out of our life even if that something is as precious to us as a hand or a foot or an eye. We must avoid those circumstances and those people that stir up evil desires and prove to be unusual sources of temptation.

Realistically, we all know that it is impossible to avoid all circumstances and occasions of temptation because temptation is all around us—in our newspapers, our magazines, our neighborhoods, our schools, our places of employment. Yet whenever we can, we should avoid those circumstances that provide unusual enticements. Scripture proclaims, "How blessed is the man who does not walk in the counsel of the wicked, nor stand in the path of sinners, nor sit in the seat of scoffers!" (Ps. 1:1). In keeping with these instructions from Psalm 1, we must not walk in the counsel, stand in the way, or sit in the seat of ungodly, sinful, and scornful people. In other words, we must not seek out, listen to, or follow the advice of people who do not have God at the center of their thoughts (Ps. 10:4; Prov. 1:7; 9:10; Eccl. 12:13).

Still further, we must not settle down and be comfortable with the practices, ways, or lifestyles of people whose lives are characterized by sins of either commission or omission. And we must not allow ourselves to spend so much time with people or ideas that overtly or covertly mock God's truth that we actually become relaxed and comfortable with them. If we do, we are in danger of becoming participants in evil with them. Indeed, we may be certain that if we do any of the things that Psalm 1 warns against, we will never be able to mortify the desires and deeds of the flesh.

APPLICATION AND DISCUSSION SUGGESTIONS

1. List the things mentioned in this chapter that we should do to help us put Romans 8:13 and Colossians 3:5–9 into practice in our lives.

2. List the passages of Scripture that support the importance of doing the things mentioned in this chapter if we want to fulfill the commands of Romans 8:13 and Colossians 3:5.

3. In the first main section of this chapter, I talk about the ripple effect of our sin. What is meant by sin's ripple effect?

4. What biblical examples of the ripple effect of sin were given in this chapter, and how do they illustrate this concept?

5. What instances of the ripple effect have you observed in the lives of others or even in your own life?

6. Explain what principle for putting sin to death is taught by Matthew 26:41.

7. What was meant by the illustration of our sinful desires' being like a fire that is burning low, or being like sediment at the bottom of a pool?

8. What principle for putting sin to death was outlined in the horse-and-buggy illustration?

9. What principle for putting sin to death was taught by Jesus in Mark 9:43–47?

10. What examples have you observed in the lives of other people, or in your own life, of times when sin occurred because these principles were neglected?

11. Do you regularly carry out the sin-killing practices described in this chapter? Try to think of specific examples of times that you did. Be ready to share them with your discussion group or counselor.

12. What practical applications for your Christian life will you make from this chapter?

9

PAY ATTENTION TO
THE SEASONS

If we are going to be successful in putting sin to death in any of the ways described so far, we must follow the counsel of Ephesians 5:11: "Do not participate in the unfruitful deeds of darkness, but instead even expose them." "Do not participate" means not sharing in ideas, perspectives, values, goals, purposes for living, or standards for life. "Darkness" represents that which is contrary to the triune God, who is Light personified (John 1:4–5, 9; 8:12; James 1:17; 1 John 1:5, 7). It also represents that which is contrary to what is taught in God's Word (Ps. 36:9; 119:105; Prov. 6:23), that which is contrary to righteousness—and therefore sinful and evil (John 3:19–21; Rom. 13:12; 2 Cor. 11:14; 1 John 2:9–10)—and that which is contrary to being a good witness for Christ (Matt. 5:14–26; John 5:35).

Avoid and Expose Darkness
and Embrace Light

A New Testament commentary on Ephesians 5:11 states: "By works of darkness are meant such things as immorality, impurity, greed, filthiness, silly talk, etc. (5:3, 4), and also those mentioned in 4:25–32; briefly, any and all works belonging to the realm of depravity and inspired by its prince. Such works are called unfruitful. They are sterile in the sense that they do not glorify God, do not win the neighbor for Christ, and do not bring inner peace or satisfaction."[1]

Exposing this kind of darkness, as Ephesians 5:11 directs, involves doing the opposite of having fellowship. At the very least, it involves not sharing, participating in, or endorsing the ideas, behaviors, perspectives, values, goals, purposes for living, or standards for life that are contrary to the things identified in the Bible as light. Christians are, in the words of Jesus, to be in the world but not of the world (John 17:15–18). They are to function as salt and light, which means, of course, that they are to be different from the world. Salt ceases to be salt when it becomes just like the food on which it is sprinkled. And light ceases to be light when it is no different from the darkness into which it shines (Matt. 5:13–16).

William Hendricksen explains, "Sin must be exposed. One is not being 'nice' to a wicked man by endeavoring to make him feel what a fine fellow he is. The cancerous tumor must be removed, not humored. It is not really an act of love to smooth things over as if the terrible evil committed by those still living in the realm of darkness is not so bad after all. . . . But how were they able to expose them . . . ? The answer which is clear from the entire context is that by means of a life of goodness and righteousness and truth (verse 9) they must reveal what vast contrast there is between the works of those who walk in light and the works of those who walk in darkness."[2]

All of this means that if we have friends who try to draw us into sin, we must not allow ourselves to cooperate or participate with them in their unbiblical activities or conversations. Rather, by the way we talk and walk, we must oppose and expose the unfruitful works of darkness. Compromise or neutrality in our relationship with and attitude toward the unfruitful works of darkness will not be good for others, and it will not be useful to us in our attempt to put the desires and deeds of the flesh to death.

A friend of mine told me that before his conversion, he drank alcoholic beverages quite heavily. After work he would often go out with the fellows from work and sit in a bar and drink excessively. When he became a Christian, he recognized that his excessive drinking was not good for him, his family, or his testimony to others. He came to the conclusion that going to bars and drinking heavily was a waste of money and time. He also realized that the atmosphere in the bar was not conducive to being a good witness for Christ. So he made the decision that he should totally abstain.

His fellow workers did not understand his sudden change of mind and kept asking him to join them. He was a young Christian and did not know how to handle this situation, but finally he told them, "Recently I have believed on the Lord Jesus Christ and become a Christian. Jesus Christ has changed my life. I have been forgiven. I now have a new relationship with God, and I now have a life filled with meaning and purpose that is quite different from how I previously lived. I'll be glad to go with you to have a cup of coffee or pick up something to eat, but now I really don't need the extra buzz I used to get from drinking. I've found so much joy and peace in my relationship with Christ that I really don't need what I used to get from drinking."

When he made that statement, this man did what Jesus said in Mark 9:43–47 that we should do to overcome sin. He acted in accordance with the instruction to cut off an offending hand, foot, or eye. When this man made the decision to stop going to bars with his friends and told them why, he was refusing to become involved in that which had been an unusual source of temptation for him. He was obeying the words of our Lord Jesus Christ in Luke 21:34: "Be on guard, so that your hearts will not be weighted down with dissipation and drunkenness and the worries of life," and he was following the instruction of the apostle Paul to mortify our evil desires.

SEASONS OF EXTRAORDINARY TEMPTATION

To succeed in obeying the biblical injunction to put sin to death in our lives, we must be especially wakeful during the seasons in our lives when we are most likely to experience extraordinary temptation. Often, a season of outward prosperity is a time of unusual temptation. The psalmist wrote, "Before I was afflicted I went astray, but now I keep Your word" (Ps. 119:67). When everything was going smoothly, when he had no major problems, the psalmist went astray. Now that he was being afflicted, he was keeping God's Word. The psalmist knew the danger of prosperity. The Bible also speaks in Proverbs 1:29–32 of how the prosperity of fools destroys them. Many people are spiritually destroyed by easy circumstances or prosperity.

One of the wisest prayers ever prayed is found in Proverbs 30:7–9. On his knees before God, this man said, "Two things I asked of You, do not refuse me before I die. . . ." What was he going to ask for? What would we ask the Lord for? First, he asked, "Keep deception and lies far from me. . . ." In other words, he wanted the Lord to take away his deceitfulness and make him a man of conviction and truth. Second, he asked, "Give me neither poverty nor riches; feed me with the food that is my portion, that I not be full and deny You and say, 'Who is the LORD?' or that I not be in want and steal, and profane the name of my God." This man, knowing the depravity of his wicked heart, was fearful of becoming too wealthy. He said, "Lord, I am afraid that if you give me riches, I will deny you." He was fearful that his riches might cause him to dishonor God by his lifestyle—by overindulgence, complacency, or neglecting the things of God. On the other hand, he said, "Don't allow me to become too poor because I can't trust myself—I may go out and steal."

This was a man who recognized that in many cases, prosperity and godliness do not go together. Though possible, it is very difficult for them to grow on the same tree. Jesus said, "How hard it will be for those who are wealthy to enter the kingdom of God! . . . Children, how hard it is to enter the kingdom of God! It is easier for a camel to go through the eye of a needle than for a rich man to enter the kingdom of God" (Mark 10:23–25). Because of this, people living in the United States ought to be especially careful. Never has a nation in the history of civilization been more blessed than the United

States. People who live here have one of the highest standards of living of any people that have ever lived.

While visiting another country, I was forcefully reminded of this when a man approached me and began to beg. Because I did not speak the language, I turned to the missionary who was with me and said, "Tell him that I'm a poor preacher and I don't have a lot of money." Instead, my missionary friend replied to me, "These people think that anyone from America is wealthy, and by their standards, we are." I have heard missionaries in other countries say the same.

People in the United States have been abundantly blessed. Consequently, they must be constantly on their guard, lest the fate of the Laodiceans come upon them. The Laodiceans of the Bible were self-satisfied, complacent, indifferent, and unconcerned about spiritual things. They tipped their hats to God. They gave God some of their time and some of their money on Sundays. They were orthodox in their doctrine, and may have even read their Bibles and spent some time in prayer. Yet as they did these things, they patted themselves on the back and boasted, "My, haven't we done a good job! Aren't we good Christians!"

Their assessment was not correct, however, because the Lord Jesus Christ said of them: "You do not know that you are wretched and miserable and poor and blind and naked. I advise you to buy from Me gold refined by fire so that you may become rich, and white garments so that you may clothe yourself, and that the shame of your nakedness will not be revealed; and eye salve to anoint your eyes so that you may see" (Rev. 3:17–18). Here was a group of people who were physically rich but spiritually poor. Though physically healthy, they were spiritually miserable and blind. They had allowed their riches and security to lull them to sleep.

In comparison with much of the rest of the world, Christians in the United States are rich. They often have large, beautiful churches with huge budgets. They have cars, TVs, houses, and luxuries galore. Let us beware, therefore, lest these material riches tempt us to indifference, complacency, looseness, and laxity in spiritual things. Let us watch, lest our abundance breed a kind of self-sufficiency. Let us be on the alert, lest our physical prosperity lead to spiritual poverty. Let us use our resources to the glory of God and for the advancement of His kingdom. Let us be down on our knees constantly asking God to help us seek first the kingdom of God and His righteousness, realizing that "from everyone who has been given much, much will be required" (Luke 12:48).

Times of prosperity are times when we are prone to be especially tempted. This fact is vividly and frequently brought before us in Scripture. If we want to put the evil deeds of the body to death, we must recognize and be especially vigilant against the temptation to sin that prosperous times provide.

SEASONS OF IDLENESS OR LEISURE CAN BE DANGEROUS TIMES

Another season in which Christians are frequently harassed by strong temptation is a time of idleness or leisure. Most of us know at least some of the details of the story of David's sin with Bathsheba. We know that what he did was very wrong and led to serious consequences. But do we know what David was doing just before he fell into this sin? Second

Samuel 11:1–2 gives us the answer: "Then it happened in the spring, at the time when kings go out to battle, that David sent Joab and his servants with him and all Israel, and they destroyed the sons of Ammon and besieged Rabbah. *But David stayed at Jerusalem.* Now when evening came *David arose from his bed* and walked around on the roof of the king's house. . . ."

David had sent his armies out to battle while he stayed home to take a vacation. The Scriptures seem to indicate that on the day when David sinned with Bathsheba, he had spent a lot of time in bed: "Now when evening came David arose from his bed. . . ." King David was taking it easy—relaxing and enjoying himself. He was not busy with the affairs of the nation; he was not in the heat of battle. No, it was during a time of leisure that David fell into that awful sin.

SEASONS OF UNUSUAL SPIRITUAL BLESSING CAN BE DANGEROUS TIMES

Still further, seasons of unusual spiritual blessing may also be times of great trial and temptation. In 1 Kings 18, Elijah was on Mount Carmel. He had a tremendous experience there: the fire of God came down, his sacrifice was consumed, and his prayer for rain was answered. It had not rained in the land for three and a half years. Yet when Elijah prayed, the rains came. It may be surprising to learn, then, what happened in the very next chapter. This same majestic Elijah, who had prayed the fire and rain of God down from heaven, went out into the wilderness and said, "Lord, I want to die. Lord, please take me home; I don't want to live anymore." He was terribly discouraged and depressed. Elijah had just experienced a season of tremendous spiritual blessing, but now he was in a time of spiritual depression.

In Mark 9, we read about the Lord's taking three disciples up to the mountain, where He is transfigured before them. Peter, James, and John came down from that mountain all aglow because they had seen the Lord in His glory. So Peter said, "Rabbi, it is good for us to be here; let us make three tabernacles, one for You, and one for Moses, and one for Elijah" (Mark 9:5). What an experience they had had! They had seen Moses and Elijah. A cloud had come out of heaven and enveloped them. They had heard God the Father speaking from heaven. Truly, they had never experienced anything like this before.

Could they ever forget it? Could they ever lose the spiritual glow and fall into sin? Yes, they could—and they did. Later in the same chapter, these very disciples begin to argue about who was going to be the greatest in the kingdom of God. Not long after their unusual blessing from God, we see them fighting over which of them will be the greatest. It sounds incredible, but it happened—and it still happens today.

We often experience our greatest temptations after a time of great spiritual blessing. For example, perhaps we have been together with God on the Lord's Day. We have heard the Word of God preached, and our hearts have been stirred—God has poured out His blessing on us. When we arise the next morning, we are still riding on the crest. And since we are still leaning on what we heard, we neglect to read our Bibles very much that day. In fact, since we spent so much time in prayer and meditation yesterday, we feel it unnecessary to pray as much either.

Why such complacency? Because we are doing quite well. We still feel the spiritual glow, so our sense of need is not great.

In the aftermath of this time of spiritual blessing, we forget that our religion is a day-by-day walk with Jesus Christ. Let us therefore be mindful, lest a time of spiritual blessing become a prelude to great spiritual danger. During such times, let us do as Jesus commanded: "Get up and pray that you may not enter into temptation" (Luke 22:46).

We would be wise to follow the counsel of Johann Freystein, expressed in this hymn:

> Rise, my soul, to watch and pray, from thy sleep
>   awaken;
> Be not by the evil day unawares o'ertaken.
> For the foe, well we know, oft his harvest reapeth while
>   the Christian sleepeth.
> Watch against the devil's snares lest asleep he find thee;
> For indeed no pains he spares to deceive and blind thee.
> Satan's prey oft are they who secure are sleeping and
>   no watch are keeping.
> Watch! Let not the wicked world with its pow'r defeat
>   thee.
> Watch lest with her pomp unfurled she betray and
>   cheat thee.
> Watch and see lest there be faithless friends to charm
>   thee, who but seek to harm thee.
> Watch against thyself, my soul, lest with grace thou
>   trifle;
> Let not self thy thoughts control nor God's mercy
>   stifle.
> Pride and sin lurk within all thy hopes to scatter; heed
>   not when they flatter.[3]

APPLICATION AND
DISCUSSION SUGGESTIONS

1. List the seasons, or times of life, mentioned in this chapter when we are most likely to experience the greatest temptations to sin.

2. Briefly give the biblical evidence for stating that each of these seasons is a time when we may experience great temptations.

3. Can you think of other times when people may be especially tempted to sin? What are they? Is there biblical evidence for thinking of these as special times of temptation?

4. Why is it helpful for us to be aware that there are times when we may be especially vulnerable to temptation?

5. What seasons have you experienced in your life? How have you been affected by the seasons in your life?

6. What examples have you observed in the lives of other people or in your own life of times when sin occurred because of a lack of vigilance during one of the seasons mentioned in this chapter?

7. Do you regularly carry out the sin-killing practices described in this chapter? Try to think of specific examples of times that you did. Be ready to share them with your discussion group or counselor.

8. What practical applications for your Christian life will you make from this chapter?

10

YOU MUST KNOW YOURSELF

Becoming acquainted with our own particular weaknesses is another key factor in putting to death that which is earthly in us. In other words, we must devote ourselves to following the counsel of 2 Corinthians 13:5, where Paul commanded us, "Examine yourselves!" If we want to have victory over evil desires, we must know ourselves.

In Mark 7:21–23 Jesus said, "For from within, out of the heart of men, proceed the evil thoughts, fornications, thefts, murders, adulteries, deeds of coveting and wickedness, as well as deceit, sensuality, envy, slander, pride and foolishness. All these evil things proceed from within and defile the man." Jesus was teaching us that we are all capable of the most heinous of sins. Any of us could fall into any of these sins because the heart is deceitful above all things and desperately wicked (Jer. 17:9).

Since we are born with hearts that are desperately wicked, any one of us is capable of a variety of sins. While this is true, it is also true that each of us is particularly susceptible to sin in certain areas. For example, all of us are proud by nature; we think more highly of ourselves than we ought to think. But some of us have more of a problem with pride than others do. Some people are widely known to be especially proud. It seems as natural for them to boast—to talk about themselves and what they have done—as it is for them to breathe.

They are like the Pharisee in Luke 18. This Pharisee came to the temple and was so proud that the Bible says that he was praying, not to God, but *to himself*. Even during a time of devotion and worship, he was all wrapped up in himself. He said, "God, I thank You that I am not like other people: swindlers, unjust, adulterers, or even like this tax collector. I fast twice a week; I pay tithes of all that I get" (Luke 18:11–12). In other words, "I am in a class all by myself." This man had a particular problem with pride.

In 3 John we read of another such man. John reported, "I wrote something to the church; but Diotrephes, who loves to be first among them, does not accept what we say. For this reason, if I come, I will call attention to his deeds which he does, unjustly accusing us with wicked words; and not satisfied with this, he himself does not receive the brethren, either, and he forbids those who desire to do so and puts them out of the church" (3 John 9–10). Pride was definitely a problem for Diotrephes. He was particularly vulnerable in this area. So it is with many of us; we love to be first among others. It seems almost natural for us to lift ourselves up and to put others down. If this is an area of particular temptation for us, we ought to know it.

Some of us have another problem, perhaps with our tempers. All of us are capable of losing our tempers, but some of us have a greater problem in this area than others. We all know people with a hair-trigger temper. Proverbs 19:19 speaks of these people who are controlled by anger, for whom anger is a characteristic feature of their lives. The Scripture says that if they get into trouble because of their anger, it is worthless to rescue them because they will soon be doing the same thing over again. It does not take much to cause them to explode.

They are like James and John, whom Jesus called the "sons of thunder." In Luke 9, Jesus and His disciples entered Samaria, but the Samaritans would not receive them. When that happened, two of the disciples said, "Lord, do You want us to command fire to come down from heaven and consume them?" (Luke 9:54). James and John said that. They had a particular problem in the area of temper, and if this is also our problem, we ought to know it so that we may be on our guard against it.

Some of us have a special problem with stubbornness. We have a problem with being argumentative. We are like Obstinate in John Bunyan's *The Pilgrim's Progress.* When the main character, Christian, left the City of Destruction, Obstinate and Pliable, who tried to persuade Christian to turn back, accompanied him. When Christian refused, Obstinate laughed at him, called him foolish, and argued with him. Obstinate had a special problem in the area of stubbornness.

He was especially contentious and combative. His mind was made up, and he would not even consider the possibility that someone else might have insights more valid than his.

Of course, Obstinate did not die with John Bunyan. He is still alive today, and he is as hard to get along with as his character in Bunyan's story. He is alive in many of us. Some of us have a contentious nature, a nature given to stubbornness. We are unwilling to even entertain the thought that any of our ideas or behaviors might be wrong and in need of change. We are bound and determined that come what may, we will do it our way because our way is the right way. We are like the man described in Proverbs 26:16, who was wiser in his own eyes than seven men who could give a discreet answer. If it is our tendency to function in this way, we ought to acknowledge it and be on guard against our stubborn, knee-jerk reactions. Until we do, it is unlikely that we will ever be able to put to death this manifestation of what is still earthly in us.

Others of us have a particular problem with gullibility: we are too agreeable. We tend to be wishy-washy; we are too easily swayed or influenced. We lack backbone and cave in too easily to others. We are like the other fellow, Pliable, who followed Christian out of the City of Destruction. When Christian refused to go back with Obstinate, Pliable said, "I'll go with you." He made up his mind on the spur of the moment, and then when difficulties arose, he changed his mind just as quickly. First he went one way, and then he went the other way. He leaped before he looked, acted before he thought, and was too easily influenced by people and problems. He was like the weather vane that turns in whatever direction the strongest wind is blowing.

Again, just as Obstinate did not die in the seventeenth century, Pliable lives on as well. He is with us today in the form of people who are tossed back and forth and blown here and there by every wind of teaching (Eph. 4:14). They are like the people of whom Jude 12 speaks, people who are susceptible to being carried about by the wind. And they are like the people that James described in James 1:6, who are "like the surf of the sea, driven and tossed by the wind." They may be interested in one thing today and something completely different tomorrow. They are convinced of one truth today and another truth tomorrow. They make promises today, but when keeping those promises becomes difficult, they renege. They are excited about seeking first the kingdom of God after a rousing sermon or a challenging book, but are bent on seeking their own kingdom when the thrill and excitement has worn off. In biblical terms, they are prone to be naive, easily taken in by smooth speech, by hype, and by flattery (Prov. 14:15–16; 26:23–25; 29:5). To their spiritual loss, they seem to lack the ability or desire to exercise biblical thinking and practice discernment.

A Very Common Area of Weakness

Another weakness to which some of us are prone is the sin of sexual immorality. All of us are capable of immorality, yet some of us have a greater problem in this area than others. Paul recognized this when he wrote to the Corinthians:

Now concerning the things about which you wrote, it is good for a man not to touch a woman. But because of immoralities, each man is to have his own wife, and each woman is to have her own husband. The husband must fulfill his duty to his wife, and likewise also the wife to her husband. The wife does not have authority over her own body, but the husband does; and likewise also the husband does not have authority over his own body, but the wife does. Stop depriving one another, except by agreement for a time, so that you may devote yourselves to prayer, and come together again so that Satan will not tempt you because of your lack of self-control. But this I say by way of concession, not of command. Yet I wish that all men were even as I myself am. However, each man has his own gift from God, one in this manner, and another in that. But I say to the unmarried and to widows that it is good for them if they remain even as I. But if they do not have self-control, let them marry; for it is better to marry than to burn with passion. (1 Cor. 7:1–9)

Paul recognized that God had not given every man the ability to abstain from marriage and the intimacy of the marriage relationship. He recognized that some people have stronger sexual desires than others do. Though he personally did not have a great problem in this area, he knew that there were those who did.

The biographies of John Bunyan, as well as the books he wrote, indicate that Bunyan did not experience great struggle in this area, though he certainly recognized that others did.

This concept that different people struggle more intensely with some sins than others do is suggested by what Bunyan wrote about Faithful's experience, in contrast with Christian's. In the section of *The Pilgrim's Progress* where Faithful shared the various temptations he had experienced since becoming a believer, he mentioned his temptation to discontentment, legalism, shame, and following his former patterns and habits of thinking and living. All of these were temptations that Christian had faced at some point as well, though there was one other that Christian had not experienced.

What was this powerful struggle that Faithful shared with Christian? As Faithful began to describe what he had "met with so far in the way," he said, "I did encounter someone whose name was Wanton; she made every effort to allure and ensnare me. . . . Unless you have already met her, you cannot imagine what a seductive tongue she has. She pressured me severely to turn aside with her, promising me all kinds of pleasure and contentment."[1]

Faithful went on to say that he had escaped Wanton's net without consenting to her desires, but it was not without great difficulty. To do so required alertness, effort, and dedication. He had to remember Scripture, make himself think of the consequences of yielding to her allurements, shut his eyes to her seductive looks, and resolutely resist her enticements. Since Scripture indicates that the temptation to sexual immorality is such a common experience, we too must be on the alert to recognize and resist Wanton's advancements. In order to put this desire and deed of the flesh to death, we must know ourselves and be prepared to follow Faithful's example in killing this temptation.

Examining and Knowing Yourself Is Crucial

We could go on and mention many other sins to which some people are particularly inclined. Perhaps at this point our particular areas of weakness have not been mentioned. Whether they have or have not, we ought to search out our own heart, know ourselves, and be aware of the areas in which we have special weaknesses in our lives.

John Owen, who is regarded by some as having more sound biblical knowledge in the tip of his little finger than most Christians do in their entire bodies, declared:

> Take heed lest you have a Jehu in you that shall make you drive furiously, or a Jonah in you that will make you ready to repine, or a David that will make you hasty in your determination as he was often in the warmth and goodness of his natural temper. He who watches not this thoroughly, who is not exactly skilled in the knowledge of himself, will never be disentangled from one temptation or another all his days. . . . Labor to know thine own frame and temper, what spirit thou art of, what associates in thine heart Satan has where corruption is strong and where grace is weak, what stronghold lusts have in thy natural constitution and the like. How many have all their comforts blasted and peace disturbed by their natural passions and peevishness! How many are rendered useless in the world by their forwardness and discontent! How many are disquieted even by their own gentleness and facility. Be ye then acquainted with thine own heart.

Though it be deep, search it. Though it be dark, inquire into it. Though it give all its distempers other names than what are their due, believe it not. Were not men utter strangers to themselves—did they not give flattering titles to their natural distempers—did they not strive rather to justify, conceal or excuse the evils of their hearts that are suited to their natural tempers and constitutions than to destroy them, and by these means keep themselves off from taking a clear and distinct view of them—it were impossible that they should all their days hang in the same briers without attempt for deliverance. Uselessness and scandal in professing Christians are branches growing constantly on this root of unacquaintedness with their own frame and temper; and how few are there who will either study them themselves or bear with those who will acquaint them with them![2]

It is generally agreed among many Christian scholars that some of the most outstanding Christians in all of church history lived during the seventeenth and eighteenth centuries. This was the time when the Puritans, or those associated with or influenced by them, lived. Unfortunately, some contemporary people misrepresent the Puritans and speak of them in derisive terms, tarring them all with the same brush. As a result, many people today think poorly of them and the era of time in which they lived. And while some of the things that have been said may be true of some of them, they are certainly not true of most of them. In the main, the Puritans were devoted, dedicated, godly, exemplary, and brilliant Christians who were very concerned about putting sin to death and living godly, holy lives.

Many of the men who lived during this period wrote voluminously, and so we have a record of what they believed. Many of them also made it a practice to keep daily journals, recording their day-by-day relationship with the Lord. Thus, even today we have George Whitefield's and David Brainerd's journals, which are still being published and still influencing people to fight sin and live holy lives. These journals reflect the fact that these men made it a practice to regularly examine themselves, in order to keep tabs on every aspect of their lives. Certainly, this was not the only reason for their exemplary godliness, but just as certainly, it was one of the reasons.

Would that more of us were as concerned about killing sin and living righteously as the Puritans were! If we were, we would regularly follow their practices of self-examination, repentance, change, and resolution to abhor what is evil and cling to what is good. Unfortunately, many people—even Christians—are reluctant to examine their own hearts because it is such a painful experience. Like people who refuse to see a doctor because they are afraid of what the doctor might find, many of us will not look into our hearts and sit under searching preaching because we are afraid of what might be uncovered. It is unpleasant to see our own sin, weakness, and wretchedness. Yet the experience is necessary if victory over sin is to be achieved.

The psalmist said, "I considered my ways and turned my feet to Your testimonies. I hastened and did not delay to keep Your commandments" (Ps. 119:59–60). When he thought about his daily life, the psalmist turned his feet to God's testimonies and he hurried to keep God's commandments. In explaining these verses, Thomas Brooks said:

> The Hebrew word that is here used for thinking, signifies to think on a man's ways accurately, advisedly, seriously, studiously, curiously. This holy man of God thought exactly and curiously on all his purposes and practice, on all his doings and sayings, on all his words and works, and finding too many of them to be short of the rule, he turned his feet to God's testimonies; having found out his errors, upon a diligent search, a strict scrutiny, he turned over a new leaf, and framed his course more exactly by rule. O Christians! You must look as well to your layings out as your layings up; you must as well forward to what you should be, as backward to what you are. Certainly Christians will never be eminent in holiness that hath many ways to behold a little holiness, and never an eye to see his further want of holiness.[3]

In the same *Treasury of David* commentary, Charles Spurgeon added these words of explanation, on the same text, from Stephen Charnock:

> Poisons may be made medicinal. Let the thoughts of old sins stir up a commotion of anger and hatred. We feel shiverings in our spirits, and a motion in our blood, at the very thought of a bitter potion we have formerly taken. Why may we not do that spiritually, which the very frame and constitution of our bodies

doth naturally, upon the calling a loathsome thing to mind? The Romans' sins were transient, but the shame was renewed every time they reflected on them: Romans 6:21, "Whereof ye are now ashamed." They reacted with detestation instead of pleasure: so should the revivings of old sins in our memories be entertained with sighs, rather than with joy. We should also manage the opportunity, so as to promote some further degrees of our conversion: "I thought on my ways, and turned my feet to thy testimonies." There is not the most hellish motion, but we may strike some sparks from it, to kindle our love to God, renew our repentance, raise our thankfulness, or quicken our obedience.[4]

What this teaches us is that real change begins with real thinking—with accurate evaluation and assessment. Many people do not change their ways because they do not ever stop to think about them. In keeping with the words of Proverbs 16:2, they assume that all their ways are right. They operate on the basis of feelings, and since they feel that their ways are right, they see no point in thinking about or evaluating themselves (Prov. 14:12). Others do not change because they do not think biblically—and therefore accurately—about their thoughts, desires, actions, or reactions. They evaluate their ways in accordance with human opinion, according to the world's standards; and if they change at all, they change so that their ways will conform to their own opinion or the judgments of their culture.

Others do what the psalmist did. They consider their ways by thinking about and evaluating them biblically. With the psalmist they say, "Therefore I esteem right all Your precepts concerning everything, I hate every false way" (Ps. 119:128). In other words, they consider everything that does not line up with God's Word to be false and in need of change. Their deep and earnest biblical thoughts lead to repentance, and repentance leads to a change in direction. Their deep and earnest biblical thoughts produce conviction, concern, and sorrow—but, more than that, a change in their thinking, desires, and conduct as they turn their feet to God's testimonies and hasten to obey His commandments. For these people, the result of biblical thinking is biblical action, and this kind of thinking and acting leads to putting the desires and deeds of the flesh to death. It leads to victory in the struggle against temptation of every kind and description.

APPLICATION AND DISCUSSION SUGGESTIONS

1. List and briefly describe the areas mentioned in this chapter in which people may have a particular weakness and therefore be more susceptible to sin.

2. Briefly give the biblical evidence for stating that these may be particular areas of weakness in which people may be more susceptible to sin.

3. Can you think of other areas of particular weakness in which people may be especially tempted to sin? Study Mark 7:21–23, Galatians 5:19–21, and 2 Timothy 3:1–6 and note the various sins mentioned in these passages to which some people may be especially vulnerable.

4. Can you think of biblical examples of people who manifested a particular vulnerability to any of the sins listed in these passages?

5. Why is it helpful for us to be aware that we may have particular propensities making us especially vulnerable to sin?

6. Identify which of these particular areas may make you especially vulnerable to sin.

7. Think back over the last week or month and identify any times when you may have been tempted to give in to sinful thoughts, desires, or actions through pride—times when you were tempted to think more highly of yourself than you ought to think.

8. Think back over the last week or month and identify any times when you may have made quick decisions without really checking out the facts (Prov. 18:13, 15).

9. Think back over the last week or month and identify any times when you were influenced by others without considering whether you were being influenced to biblical thinking or living.

10. Think back over the last week or month and identify times when you admitted that you were discouraged by difficulties and hardships and were ready to renege on a commitment you had made.

11. Think back over the last week and identify times when you did or said what was right even though you knew others would not approve or appreciate what you did or said.

12. Go to a trusted and courageous friend and ask him or her to evaluate you in terms of any of the propensities mentioned in Mark 7:21–23, Galatians 5:19–21, 2 Timothy 3:1–6 (pride, fear, worry, gullibility, discernment, fulfilling your commitments, continuing to do what is right even though others do not approve, etc.), or any of the areas of sin mentioned in this chapter.

13. What point was being made in this chapter by contrasting the life of Faithful with the life of Christian in *The Pilgrim's Progress*? How would it appear that they were different? What can we learn from this example?

14. What do we learn from the example of the psalmist in Psalm 119:59–60 about putting sin to death in our lives?

15. Why is it that people seem to hesitate to examine themselves?

16. Do you regularly carry out the sin-killing practices described in this chapter? Try to think of specific examples of times that you did. Be ready to share them with your discussion group or counselor.

17. What practical applications for your Christian life will you make from this chapter?

11

DON'T LISTEN TO SIN'S SALES PITCH

M any years ago, my wife and I got an advertisement in the mail from a photography studio. The company wanted to send a photographer to our home and take pictures of our children, offering one picture for a nominal fee and claiming that the purchase of additional pictures was completely optional. Since we had not had pictures of the children taken for some time, we decided to accept the offer. At the same time, we also decided that we would buy only one picture. So an appointment was made and the photographer came to the house and took the pictures.

A few weeks later, we got a call from the photographer saying that the pictures were ready and that he would like to bring them to the house for a showing. Before he came, Carol and I reminded ourselves that we were going to buy only one picture. The photographer came with his suitcase and pulled out many different pictures—large, medium, small, and wallet-sized pictures. He even had some slides that required a special kind of viewer that he also had with him for sale.

He went through his sales pitch and told us how nice the pictures were and how important it was for us to have them. When we replied that we wanted only one of the pictures, he launched into a full-out, no-holds-barred sales pitch. He tried to convince us that we really needed the whole package. He attempted to woo us by telling us how inexpensive the pictures were (they were not), how wonderful the pictures were, how beautiful our children were (they were), and what these pictures would mean to our children, their grandparents, and us in the future.

Then he proceeded to do everything he could to warn us against rejecting his offer. He implied that if we did not buy his pictures, we would be sorry in the future. He even implied that if we got only one picture, we must not really love or value our children. In a word, he pulled out all the stops, and by the time the photographer left, we had bought a whole stack of pictures, including the slides and the slide viewer.

After the man left, I said to my wife, "Why did we do that? Why did we allow him to sell us all those pictures?" "I don't know," she answered. In fact, we agreed that the pictures were not even that good. So where did we go wrong? We made our mistake when we did not stop him the moment he began his sales pitch. The moment he opened his mouth to try to sell us more pictures, we should have said, "We want only one. You told us that we could buy one picture for a small fee. We are buying that picture and no more. We're sorry that it cost you some time and effort, but we didn't make you come. We believed that you meant what you said, and now it would seem that you are going back on your word. You're implying that if we don't buy more pictures, we're being bad parents. But there is more to good parenting than taking and buying pictures. In fact, we would like to tell you what good parenting really involves . . ." Unfortunately, we did not do that. Instead of stopping him cold, we allowed him to slowly tempt us beyond what we were prepared to resist.

IMMEDIATELY RESIST
ANY UNGODLY SALES PITCH

This is where we often go wrong with our evil desires. This is how we often fall into temptation. We allow our evil desires, the weaknesses of our flesh, the world, and the devil to give us their sales pitches. We do not immediately say "no" to ungodly thoughts, desires, and feelings. When desires flare up, we do not immediately stamp them out. We do not immediately resist temptations. Instead, we allow sin to give us a sales pitch that we are unprepared to resist. Our resolve is weakened, and we fall because we never really prepared ourselves to stand firm.

This is how Eve made her mistake. In Genesis 3, Eve allowed the devil to give her his sales pitch. The moment the devil showed up in the form of a serpent, she should have said, "Goodbye, Mr. Serpent; I don't want anything to do with you. I don't want to hear a word you have to say. I have already heard from God, and the matter is settled. We might as well not discuss it." But Eve did not do that. Even though at that point she was a godly woman living in a perfect environment, she allowed the devil to give her his sales pitch and quickly found out that she was no match for him.

The Bible describes what she did in this way: "When the woman saw that the tree was good for food, and that it was a delight to the eyes, and that the tree was desirable to make one wise, she took from its fruit and ate . . ." (Gen. 3:6). Now, this tree had been in the garden all along, but because of the devil's convincing sales pitch, suddenly Eve saw the tree in a whole new light. Now that she thought about it, its fruit did look good to eat, and best of all, the devil had said that it would make her wise. So as a result of listening rather than resisting, "she took from its fruit and ate; and she gave also to her husband with her, and he ate" (Gen. 3:6).

Where did Eve go wrong? Eve did not resist the first inclination, or thought, of sin. She allowed the devil to give her his sales pitch, and she was no match for him.

FOLLOW JOB'S EXAMPLE

Turning to the book of Job, we see how Job did the very opposite thing, and as result of his immediate resistance, he experienced victory over a powerful temptation. In the first chapter of this book, Job encountered some terrible problems. In one day, many horrible things happened to him. The Scripture says that when Job was in his house one day:

> A messenger came to Job and said, "The oxen were plowing and the donkeys feeding beside them, and the Sabeans attacked and took them. They also slew the servants with the edge of the sword, and I alone have

escaped to tell you." While he was still speaking, another also came and said, "The fire of God fell from heaven and burned up the sheep and the servants and consumed them, and I alone have escaped to tell you." While he was still speaking, another also came and said, "The Chaldeans formed three bands and made a raid on the camels and took them and slew the servants with the edge of the sword, and I alone have escaped to tell you." While he was still speaking, another also came and said, "Your sons and your daughters were eating and drinking wine in their oldest brother's house, and behold, a great wind came from across the wilderness and struck the four corners of the house, and it fell on the young people and they died, and I alone have escaped to tell you." (Job 1:14–19)

Try to imagine this scene and put yourself in Job's place. All of these things happened not over a period of years, or even weeks, but in a single day. Job lost all his earthly possessions, all his servants, all his animals, and all his children. In a period of about twenty-four hours, Job, a relatively old man (his children were grown and living in their own houses), lost most of what he had worked hard to accumulate. With no insurance and probably not much of a bank account, Job really had nothing.

What would we have done in this situation? Would we have lashed out against God? Would we have given vent to the bitterness and venom in our hearts? Would we have lashed out against others with words of accusation, acrimony, and self-pity? Would we have become extremely depressed? Scripture indicates that Job did none of these things.

The Bible says, "Then Job arose and tore his robe and shaved his head, and he fell to the ground and worshiped. He said, 'Naked I came from my mother's womb, and naked I shall return there. The LORD gave and the LORD has taken away. Blessed be the name of the LORD.' Through all this Job did not sin nor did he blame God" (Job 1:20–22). This was a godly man.

Part of Job's response—tearing his robe and shaving his head—indicates that he did experience great sadness and grief. He certainly must have been tempted to respond in ungodly ways, but he resisted that temptation. Instead of giving vent to bitterness, he immediately went into the presence of God and worshiped. Though he did not deny his feelings, neither did he allow his feelings to control him. Rather, he immediately exerted control over his emotions by reminding himself of biblical truth and then by spending time in worship. This is the kind of response we ought to have when we are tempted to sin. We must immediately flee into the presence of God, remind ourselves of biblical truth, and then spend time in worship and communion with the Lord.

In Job 2, Job encountered more difficulty. The Bible records, "Then Satan went out from the presence of the LORD and smote Job with sore boils from the sole of his foot to the crown of his head. And he took a potsherd to scrape himself while he was sitting among the ashes. Then his wife said to him, 'Do you still hold fast your integrity? Curse God and die!' " (Job 2:7–9). Imagine what it must have felt like to be covered head to toe in tremendously painful boils. To make matters worse, Satan then used Job's wife to tempt him to sin against God. She told him, "Job, lash out against God. It's not fair what He has done to you, so let Him know how upset you are. Just let Him have it. Tell Him how horrible He is for treating you this way."

But notice Job's immediate response in verse 10: "But he said to her, 'You speak as one of the foolish women speaks. Shall we indeed accept good from God and not accept adversity?' In all this Job did not sin with his lips." Immediately, when the temptation came, what did Job do? Did he mull it over in his mind? Did he say, "I'll think about your suggestion. I'll meditate on it and see if it's a good idea." No, Job immediately resisted his wife's counsel. He renounced it, and this is one of the reasons that Job had victory over his temptation.

What Job did is what we ought to do when tempted by our evil desires, by other people, or by unpleasant, painful circumstances. We ought to immediately resist the temptation to internally or externally respond to our problems in an ungodly, sinful way. The time to deal with temptation is not after we have thought about it unbiblically for a period of time or after we have allowed a spark of anger to be fanned into such an intense flame that it scorches someone else. The time to deal with the problem of temper is at the very moment we feel the heat rising.

The time to deal with bitterness or malice is not after we have stewed about it for a week, two weeks, or a month. By that time we have so much hatred and animosity and bitterness in our hearts toward that other person that we may find it difficult even to be around him or her. The time to deal with bitterness or malice is when we first begin to feel it arising. At the moment we begin to feel hurt or angry, we ought to turn to God and say, "O God, I'm starting to think unbiblical thoughts about this person. Please help me to bring my thoughts under control and make them obedient to Jesus Christ [2 Cor. 10:4–5]. By your grace and with your help, I commit myself to practicing a love that is patient and kind, that is not proud, that does not behave in a rude or discourteous way, that will not keep a record of wrongs done to it, and that thinks no evil [1 Cor. 13:4–8]. I also commit myself to filling my mind with things that are pure, right, just, honorable, lovely, worthy of praise, and pleasing in Your sight [Phil. 4:8]. Lord, this is my commitment; please help me to keep it."

The best time to deal with the problem of slander or gossip is not after we have spent two hours on the telephone sharing all the juicy tidbits of someone else's unpleasant behavior or words. Rather, the time to deal with that particular temptation is the moment we feel tempted to open our mouths. We ought to be constantly praying the prayer of the psalmist, "Set a guard, O Lord, over my mouth; keep watch over the door of my lips" (Ps. 141:3). We ought to ask God to help us to "let no unwholesome word proceed from [our] mouth[s], but only such a word as is good for edification . . . , so that it will give grace to those who hear" (Eph. 4:29).

Proverbs 18:21 says that the power of death and life is in the tongue. We can ruin another person's reputation, his character, and even—to a degree—his Christian service by the way that we use our tongues. Let us, then, deal with the problem of gossip or slander at the very moment we are tempted to say something we ought not to say. Let us immediately kill this sin and replace it with speech that is wholesome and edifying.

The best time to deal with deceitfulness is not after we have lied, but the moment we are tempted to lie in any of its many forms. In many places, the Bible highlights the fact that deceitfulness is a very common practice among human beings. Psalm 58:3 indicates that deceitfulness is as natural to a child as breathing: "The wicked are estranged from the womb; these who speak lies go astray from birth."

A child must be taught many things, but lying is not one of them. The practice of lying begins early and, in most cases, is very obvious when done by a child. With practice and age, however, we sharpen this skill and often use it in more subtle and sophisticated ways so that it is not as easily recognizable. Nevertheless, though we become more creative in disguising our deceitfulness, lying is still a very common behavior among adults. Politicians, businessmen, employees, employers, lawyers, husbands, wives—everyone, at one time or another, seems to misrepresent the truth when it is to their advantage.

Romans 1:18 tells us that by nature men "suppress the truth." Verse 25 of the same chapter tells us that exchanging the truth of God for a lie is a given for unredeemed humanity. In other words, it is easier and more natural for unbelievers to believe the lies of Satan than the truth of God. In Romans 3:9–18, where God describes the natural condition of all human beings, we are told that deceitfulness is one of the main sinful practices of men.

This propensity to deceive is emphasized in the Bible by countless examples as well. If we look almost anywhere in the Bible, we will find examples of people who lied. Cain lied in Genesis 4, Abraham lied in Genesis 12 and 20, and Isaac lied in Genesis 26. Jacob lied in Genesis 27 (and also on several other occasions), the brothers of Joseph lied in Genesis 37, and Potiphar's wife lied in Genesis 39. All of these lies are found within the book of Genesis, and we have not even begun to consider the rest of the Bible.

Recording these many statements and examples of lying in Scripture is God's way of highlighting the fact that deceitfulness is a serious and common problem with us. Lying, in the form of flagrantly saying something that is not based on fact and is therefore false, is one common method (as Jacob did with his father in Genesis 27). But there are many other forms of lying: exaggeration (making much more out of something than it really is, as Ananias and Sapphira did in Acts 5), evasion (as Cain did with the Lord in Genesis 4), misrepresentation (as Satan did with Eve about the Lord in Genesis 3), and making promises that are not kept (as God accuses some men of doing in Malachi 2:15–17).

Another very common method of deception is lying in order to save face, or to excuse ourselves from responsibility, or to make ourselves look better than we really are, or to make others look worse than they really are. In Mark 7:21–23, lying is listed as one of the things that is found in our hearts, easily comes out of our hearts, and is expressed in our lives as well as by our mouths. In Colossians 3:9, Paul indicated that even though a person may be a genuine Christian, he may still have a tendency to be deceitful. And since this is true, Paul specifically mentioned lying as an "evil practice" that must be put to death.

To put the sin of deceitfulness—in any of its forms—to death, we must recognize that it is a sin and, more than that, a sin to which all of us are prone. Then we must fill our minds and hearts with God's perspective on lying and truthfulness. To do this, we must memorize verses about deception, we must be on guard against it, and we must determine to immediately resist the temptation whenever it occurs. Finally, we must commit ourselves to developing the practice of putting away falsehood and speaking the truth to one another (Eph. 4:25; Col. 3:9). To kill this sin, we must never minimize its seriousness, we must never allow ourselves to think that we could never sin in this way, and we must be alert and seek God's help to become people who are truth-bearers and truth-tellers.

Most of us, even though we are Christians, have encountered the temptation to lie and even succumbed to it on many occasions. We may be sure that what has happened to us in the past will happen again. We can count on facing this temptation again. Therefore, let us determine to prepare ourselves ahead of time to resist. We must be ready to fight against temptation because victory over deception or any other sin does not happen automatically.

No one wins their battles over sin while sitting in a recliner, relaxed or fast asleep. Victories are won only when we realize that temptation is a given, when we prepare ourselves ahead of time to resist, and as we immediately resist when it comes our way. Being ready to act and following through is a vital part of fulfilling Romans 8:13 and Colossians 3:5.

APPLICATION AND DISCUSSION SUGGESTIONS

1. List the things mentioned in this chapter that we should do to help us put Romans 8:13 and Colossians 3:5–9 into practice in our lives.

2. List the Scriptures that support the importance of doing the things mentioned in this chapter if we want to actually fulfill the commands found in Romans 8:13 and Colossians 3:5.

3. What was the main point of the photographer illustration in the beginning of this chapter?

4. What truth about putting sin to death can we learn from Eve's experience with the serpent in Genesis 3? Describe the details of what happened to Eve.

5. What can we learn about putting sin to death from the example of Job, in Job 1 and 2? Describe the details of what happened to Job and how he responded.

6. Why is it true that the best time to resist temptation is when it first seeks to entice you? Study Proverbs 17:14 and James 1:13–15 and note the relevance of these passages to the main idea of this chapter.

7. What particular temptations into which people are very likely to fall were mentioned in this chapter?

8. Use a concordance to help you list and explain several Scripture verses that deal with the sins mentioned in this chapter.

9. Do you agree that the temptations mentioned in this chapter are very common?

10. What can we learn about the sin of deceitfulness from Colossians 3:9?

11. What reason is there for believing that these are very common temptations?

12. Do you regularly carry out the sin-killing practices described in this chapter? Try to identify specific examples of times that you did. Be ready to share them with your discussion group or counselor.

13. What practical applications for your Christian life will you make from this chapter?

12

LEARN FROM FAILURES

As mentioned in chapter 6, the Bible makes it clear that no Christian, even one as godly as the apostle Paul, is successful in completely and always putting sin to death. First John 1:8 pounds this truth home: "If we say that we have no sin, we are deceiving ourselves and the truth is not in us." As we progress in the Christian life, we can sin less, but we will never be sinless this side of heaven. If we compare the practice of putting sin to death to a baseball game, we must say that no Christian always hits a home run. No Christian always plays a perfect game.

By God's grace, as we implement the things described in this book, we can experience more and more victory, though with Paul we will always have to say, "Not that I have already obtained it or have already become perfect, but I press on so that I may lay hold of that for which also I was laid hold of by Christ Jesus" (Phil. 3:12). According to Romans 8:29, God laid hold of us so that we would be conformed to the image of His Son, so that Christ might be totally formed in us. In Philippians 3:12, Paul was saying, "I'm not there yet. I'm making progress, but I still have a long way to go, so I'm pressing on 'toward the goal for the prize of the upward call of God in Christ Jesus' [Phil. 3:14]." In other words, he was continuing to put off his sinful desires and constantly striving to be more like the holy Son of God, his Savior.

Is our attitude a reflection of Paul's attitude? Is our commitment similar to Paul's commitment? Do we understand that we have not attained the goal God has for us: to be perfect like Christ? Christ was holy, harmless, and undefiled (Heb. 7:26). He always resisted sin, and He always lived a righteous life both outwardly and inwardly. God has saved us so that we might be conformed to His image, so that He might be the firstborn among many brethren (Rom. 8:29). Along with that of the apostle Paul, our goal in life should be to conform to the image of Christ. In this world, we will never completely attain that goal, but we should always be pressing toward it. And we will make progress toward it as we learn more and more about how Romans 8:13 and Colossians 3:5 teach us to live.

Learn from Your Own Failures

In striving to be conformed to Christ's image, we must not allow our failures to discourage or deter us from pressing on. When we fail to put what is earthly in us to death, we should confess and repent of our sins and then determine to move on. We must never allow our past or present failures to hinder us from pressing on. Part of not being hindered by our failures means that we should forget the things that are behind (Phil. 3:13). Yet learning from our sins and failures and even the sins and failures of others can be very helpful in killing the desires and deeds of our flesh.

In Joshua 6, the Israelites went against the city of Jericho and won a great victory. The walls of Jericho came tumbling down. This stunning victory makes what happens next, in Joshua 7, all the more remarkable. These same people experienced a great defeat when they went up against the little town of Ai. After this happened, we find Joshua on his face before God in consternation and confusion. He bemoaned what had occurred, he was sad, he was discouraged, and he actually complained to God. He basically said to the Lord, "Why did You bring us here? Did You bring us out here to destroy us? Lord, why did You allow this to happen?"

What was God's response to Joshua? He came to Joshua and said, in effect, "Joshua, get up off your face. What are you doing down there, anyway? Stand up on your feet. Instead of moaning and complaining, why are you not searching out the reason for your defeat? Why are you not looking at your failure and trying to find out why it happened? Let Me tell you why you failed. You failed because there is a sinner in the camp. Moreover, I want you to know that if you deal with this man properly, you can go against Ai again and I will give you victory." And that is exactly what happened. When Joshua saw the problem, understood why the Israelites had failed, and dealt with it in God's way, Ai melted before them.

In similar fashion, when we sin, we ought to go down on our faces before God, confessing and repenting of our sin. But let us not stop there; let us also get up off our faces and begin to think, "Where did I go wrong? Where did I make my mistakes, and why did I go down in defeat?" We must examine our failures. We must analyze them and learn from them.

Perhaps, as we assess our failure to put sin to death, we will discover that we failed because we have neglected sin-killing practices. Thinking back, we may remember that we have failed to maintain a vital, consistent, and practical quiet time with the Lord. Last Sunday, our heart was full and blessed by the services. We went to bed a little late that night and got up a little late the next morning. As a result, we had just enough time to dress, eat breakfast, and get to work on time. We neglected our usual morning time with the Lord. That evening, we were busy with chores. We watched a TV show that we had been looking forward to. As we went to bed, we rationalized that since we had such a tremendous time with the Lord yesterday, what difference would it make if we skipped our quiet time on Monday?

Then Tuesday morning, when the alarm went off, we were so tired that instead of getting up and having devotions, we slept in an extra half hour. Again we made the excuse that we did not get enough sleep and that we would be too tired to do a good job at work. And again, when evening came, instead of making time to meet with the Lord, we allowed family issues, phone calls, and more chores to interfere. By 11:00, it was too late to do anything effective and meaning-ful—it would have to wait until Wednesday. But Wednesday morning was much the same, except that we felt better that day knowing that we would be going to prayer meeting in the evening. At least we would have a time of Bible study and prayer at church, if not by ourselves.

As we analyze what happened to our week, we begin to realize that this kind of thing has happened all too frequently over extended periods of our life. As we follow the example of the psalmist and think on our ways (Ps. 119:59), we may begin to wonder whether our loss of a sense of God's presence and our rather frequent failure to put our sinful desires to death may have something to do with our failure to maintain a quiet time with the Lord. We may become aware of the fact that we have not been faithfully memorizing or meditating on Scripture. We have not been praying without ceasing. We have not disciplined ourselves to be still and know that God is God. We have not reflected enough on the meaning and purpose of Christ's death on our behalf or on the indwelling presence of the Holy Spirit.

After this time of serious reflection, we may ask ourselves, "Could it be that I allowed myself to think, act, speak, and feel the way that I have because I have failed to regularly commune with God? Could it be that I have experienced barrenness in my life because I have not regularly delighted in and meditated on God and His Word [Josh. 1:8–9; Ps. 1:2–3]? Could it be that I did not bring every thought into captivity and make it obedient to Christ because I did not keep my mind focused on God and His Word? Could it be that this is why, when temptations present themselves, I seem to be going out to do battle without an awareness of the Lord's presence and power? Is this why I have failed to put sin to death in my life?"

Or perhaps, as we analyze the reasons for our failures, we begin to wonder whether we failed because we did not realize the seriousness of sin, as described in Part 1 of this book. Perhaps we did not think seriously enough about the effect of our sin on Christ's reputation, on other people, or even on ourselves, as described in chapters 7 and 8 of this book.

We may become aware that we were not walking in the Spirit, but rather grieving and even quenching the Holy Spirit and His ministry in us. Perhaps we did not realize that our sin was going to get so complicated and involved, causing all the problems that it did. We never thought about the fact that it might snowball, picking up speed and influence in our lives. We never anticipated that one sin would lead to another and another and on and on.

Or perhaps we were not careful to watch, as described in chapters 8 and 9. We came into a situation unaware, our guard down, and before we knew it, we had lost control of our temper. We became involved in doing something that we should not have done. Why? Because we were not careful to watch out for our own particular weaknesses. We were not guarding against occasions and circumstances that could lead us into sin. We were not aware of the seasons in which we were most likely to be tempted.

When we fail to put sin to death, we must never simply excuse or ignore it. We must go back and examine what was going on in our lives when sin took hold of us. We have to make it a point to learn from our failures. Any astute businessman would do the same. If he was losing a great deal of money or if a product was not selling, he would never sit back, fold his hands, and say, "Well, I can't do anything about that." Never! He would investigate the matter to find out what the problem was. He would go back and learn from his failures.

So it must be with us in our battle with sin. We must learn from our failures if we would have victory over it.

Learn from the Failures of Others

It is helpful to learn not only from our own failures, but also from the failures of others. The Bible says in Romans 15:4, "For whatever was written in earlier times was written for our instruction, so that through perseverance and the encouragement of the Scriptures we might have hope." Indeed, many of the things in the Word of God were recorded so that we would not make the same mistakes.

In 1 Corinthians 10:5, Paul said concerning the Israelites, "Nevertheless, with most of them God was not well-pleased; for they were laid low in the wilderness." The next verse continues, "Now these things happened as examples for us, so that we would not crave evil things as they also craved." These things were written, Paul said, that we might learn from the Israelites' experience.

In verse 11 Paul wrote, "Now these things happened to them as an example, and they were written for our instruction, upon whom the ends of the ages have come." In other words, God has included these accounts in His Word so that we can go to the Word of God and learn how to avoid failures. As we read these biblical accounts, we ought to ask ourselves, "Why did the Israelites fall into sin as they did? What were the reasons for their failures? What can I learn from their experience so that I will not do the same thing?" When we read about David's sin, we should ask, "Why did David fail as he did? How can I avoid sinning as he did?"

When we read in 1 Kings 19 about Elijah's failure, we should ask ourselves, "Why was Elijah defeated as he was? How did that happen so soon after the tremendous experiences he had on Mount Carmel? Why did he run away and say, 'Lord, I want to die'? Why was he not able, at that point in his life, to put his earthly desires to death?" If we want to avoid the same kind of failure, we should make it a point to learn from Elijah's defeat.

We ought to think about the prophet Jonah, who likewise did not put to death what was earthly in him. In chapter 1, when God told Jonah to do something, he ran away and got himself into all kinds of trouble. Later, after God had dealt severely with him, he reluctantly did as God had asked. He went to Nineveh and preached to the people, but when they responded in a way that Jonah did not like, he fell into sin again. Instead of putting to death the sinful desires and deeds of his body by the power of the Spirit, he became angry and went out and sat down under a gourd tree. There he moaned, pouted, and indulged his anger, even lashing out against the Lord. He was depressed and wanted to die because things had not worked out in a way that pleased him.

When we read that story, we should pause to ask some questions for our personal edification. We should be thinking, "Why was Jonah angry? Why did he sin like that? What was his problem? Why did Jonah not put to death the deeds of the flesh? What can I learn from Jonah's story that will help me to avoid doing what he did?"

In order to put sin to death, we must be constantly going to the Word of God to learn from the failures of others. And having learned from them, we should take note and determine to avoid making the same mistakes.

APPLICATION AND DISCUSSION SUGGESTIONS

1. List the things mentioned in this chapter that we should do to help us put Romans 8:13 and Colossians 3:5–9 into practice in our lives.

2. List the Scriptures that support the importance of doing the things mentioned in this chapter if we would actually fulfill the commands of Romans 8:13 and Colossians 3:5.

3. What can we learn about putting sin to death from the experience of the Israelites when they lost a battle with Ai? Describe what happened on this occasion.

4. What truths about putting sin to death can we learn from the experience of the Israelites, as described in 1 Corinthians 10:1–11 and Numbers 14?

5. What can we learn about putting sin to death from the example of Elijah in 1 Kings 18 and 19? Describe the details of what happened to Elijah and how he responded.

6. What can we learn about putting sin to death from the example of Jonah? Describe the details of what happened to Jonah and how he responded.

7. What can we learn about putting sin to death from the example of David in 2 Samuel 11 and 12? Describe the details of what happened to David and how he responded.

8. Do you regularly carry out the sin-killing practices described in this chapter? Try to identify specific examples of times that you did. Be ready to share them with your discussion group or counselor.

9. What practical applications for your Christian life will you make from this chapter?

13

CONCLUDING LESSONS ON KILLING SIN

As we concluded our last chapter, we spent some time analyzing several examples of people who failed to mortify or kill what was earthly that remained in them. In this chapter, we will do two things. First, we will carefully examine a time in the life of the apostle Peter when he failed to put his evil desires and deeds to death. Second, we will consider some concluding remarks about killing our sin before it kills us.

I want to begin this chapter by doing a rather intensive case study of an episode in the life of Peter. Let's focus on it as it is described for us in Matthew 26:30–75.

LEARN FROM PETER'S FAILURE

As described in Matthew 26, Peter was, at this point in his life, unquestionably a dedicated disciple of Jesus Christ. He was a child of God who loved Christ and wanted to serve

Him, and yet in this instance he denied Jesus. Or, in keeping with the truth of Romans 8:13 and Colossians 3:5, he failed to put to death the deeds of the body. Why did he fail in this way? Why did Peter wander away from the Lord?

As is often the case, it did not happen overnight. In order to understand what happened to Peter, we need to think carefully about the events that took place on the eve of our Lord's crucifixion. In Matthew 26, we find that Peter was defeated by sin not because there was anything lacking in his dedication. There was nothing wrong with Peter's devotion to Jesus Christ. In verse 31, Jesus warned Peter and the other disciples that they were all going to fall away. In response, Peter said, "Even though all may fall away because of You, I will never fall away" (Matt. 26:33).

Stating that he would never fall away and even suggesting that his commitment was deeper than anyone else's was a strong statement. In verse 35, after Jesus predicted that Peter would indeed fall away as the others, Peter reaffirmed his dedication in even stronger terms: "Even if I have to die with You, I will not deny You." From this we can see that there was nothing wrong with Peter's dedication to Christ. Could he have stated it in a more resolute way?

What Wasn't Wrong with Peter

But Peter's statement not only indicated a resolute dedication; it indicated unqualified dedication as well. He did not say, "I will be true to You up to a point, but if it goes beyond that point, then I'm going to turn away." No, Peter said, "Lord, even if I have to die with You, I will be true to You." That was an unqualified dedication.

In addition to being resolute and unqualified, Peter's dedication was also sincere. In Luke 22, when the soldiers came to take Jesus, Peter immediately pulled his sword. His first response was to do anything he could to defend Jesus. When Peter made that bold move, he knew that he was facing professional soldiers who knew how to fight. He knew that they were extremely skilled at using a sword, though Peter himself, being a fisherman, likely knew very little. But Peter's dedication was so sincere that despite his lack of skill and despite the fact that the disciples were clearly outnumbered by the soldiers, he was ready to fight. When Peter said, "I am willing to die with You," it is obvious that he meant it.

Clearly, there was nothing wrong with Peter's dedication. It was unqualified, it was determined, and it was sincere. And yet the fact remains that Peter failed—and failed miserably. The crucial lesson from this episode is that while good resolutions may be helpful, they are not enough.

This fact is illustrated by what Peter did in Matthew 26:69–75. This passage describes how Peter failed to put to death that which was earthly in him and how he allowed his feelings to control him and impel him to do that which was blatantly sinful. I would like to call attention to three things about Peter's failure. First, the passage indicates that Peter's failure was deliberate: he did not simply slip into it. His failure was not an accident; it did not "just happen." It was a deliberate denial of Jesus Christ, and thus, it was deliberate sin.

We know this because there was a space of time between each of Peter's three denials. This means that Peter had time to think about what was going on and what he should do. Besides that, Jesus had recently warned them that both He and all His disciples were going to face difficulty. Jesus had also specifically warned Peter that he would be put in situations in which he would be tempted to deny Him. Jesus had told Peter that Satan wanted to sift him like wheat. So Peter had time to think and plan. He was not taken unawares. His denial was a deliberate one.

More than that, we can see that Peter's denial was progressive. In verse 70 we read, "But he denied it before them all, saying, 'I do not know what you are talking about.' " In verse 72, "again he denied it with an oath, 'I do not know the man.' " Then, in verse 74, "he began to curse and swear, 'I do not know the man!' " From these statements we may surely conclude that his failure was progressive; one sin led to another.

Peter's denial began with an "I don't know what you're talking about" kind of statement. The second time, it got more involved. He used an oath and said again that he did not know Christ. Finally, he began to curse and swear. Being a fisherman, Peter knew some curse words. He knew the vulgar, ungodly language of the day, and when he was put in a difficult, potentially embarrassing, and even dangerous situation, these curse words flowed easily out of his mouth. Once the sluice gate of sin was opened, Peter added sin to sin.

Yet in addition to the fact that Peter's denial was deliberate and progressive, the passage indicates that his failure was only temporary. This whole period of denial lasted for no more than four or five hours. Luke 22:61–62 tells us that after Peter denied Christ, "the Lord turned and looked at Peter. And Peter remembered the word of the Lord, how He had told him,

'Before a rooster crows today, you will deny Me three times.'
And he went out and *wept bitterly*."

Peter broke down in great sobs of sorrow, guilt, conviction, and repentance. He experienced the kind of godly sorrow that leads to repentance (2 Cor. 7:9–11). Later, after Christ had been raised from the dead, Jesus met with Peter to assure him of His forgiveness and to recommission him for service (John 21:15–19). The book of Acts tells us the rest of the story, indicating that Peter's serious failure was indeed both temporary and forgiven.

Failure to put sin to death was certainly not the general trend of Peter's life. He did fail on this occasion, and we are told in other passages of Scripture that he failed on other occasions as well (Acts 10:9–16; Gal. 2:11–14). But failure to put the deeds of the body to death was not the general trend of his life. We can be sure from the book of Acts and his own epistles (1 and 2 Peter) that though Peter sometimes failed, his failures were only temporary. Afterward, he always repented and worked on changing.

Why Did Peter Fail to Put Sin to Death on This Occasion?

The overall trend of Peter's life was a godly one, yet Scripture indicates that there were times when Peter did not put that which was earthly in himself to death. One of these times was clearly described in Matthew 26, so let us look to see what we can learn from this failure by an otherwise very godly man, that we might avoid making the same mistakes that he made.

Why did Peter, on this occasion, fail to put to death the deeds of the body? In general, I think that we can make a safe and biblically supported argument that Peter failed to do many of the things mentioned in this book as important practices for killing sin.

1. Obviously, at this point in Peter's life, he did not have the fullness of teaching that we now have about the Holy Spirit. Nor did he have the fullness of teaching on the meaning and purpose of Christ's death, as mentioned in chapter 7 of this book. Most of the teaching on these subjects is found in the epistles inspired by the Holy Spirit and did not come about until after Christ actually died, was resurrected, and ascended into heaven. Certainly Peter had some information on these truths, but it is unlikely that he had the fullness of teaching that we now have.

2. He did not focus enough on how his failure to put the sins he committed in Matthew 26 to death would reflect on the reputation of our Lord Jesus Christ or on other people, including the other disciples, as described in chapter 8 of this book.

3. He certainly did not think enough about the seriousness of his sins, as described in chapters 1 to 5 of this book.

4. There is no evidence to suggest that he took seriously the exhortation of Jesus to watch and stay on the alert against temptation. It appears that he was spiritually drowsy.

5. Likewise, the biblical record does not suggest that Peter was practicing Ephesians 5:11: "Do not participate in

the unfruitful deeds of darkness, but instead even expose them."

6. It appears that in spite of the warnings of Jesus about Satan's trying to sift him and about the suffering that he was about to experience, Peter was not particularly thinking about the fact that he might soon be entering a season of unusual temptation. He probably did not even think about the fact that there *are* seasons in which we are more likely to be tempted, as described in chapters 8 and 9.

7. Still further, an examination of Peter's life to this point gives no indication that Peter was especially alert to or concerned about his own particular areas of weakness, as described in chapter 10.

8. Moreover, it appears that Peter listened to the ungodly sales pitch of his own heart and of others without immediately resisting. When the sales pitch came, did he immediately recognize its ungodly source and refuse to give it a moment's consideration? Nothing in the text supports the idea that he did.

9. Peter had failed previously, as recorded in Matthew 16:21–23 and 17:1–13. Was he particularly aware of his propensity to be too self-confident and to speak and act without really thinking? Was he aware of his tendency to be too concerned about what people thought? Was he on guard against his fear of suffering? Had Peter really given much thought to his own weaknesses? Had he really thought through the reasons for his previous failures and learned lessons that would help him to resist in the present and future?

Had Peter studied the accounts of others who had failed to put sin to death and learned lessons about how he could avoid doing the same thing from them? Perhaps he had, but if so, nothing in Scripture would warrant such a conclusion.

10. As we look at the Word of God, there is every reason to believe that Peter failed because he was overconfident in himself and in his own abilities. This conclusion is implied in what we have already discussed, but it is so important that I want to give it some special attention. Overconfidence in self is always a spiritually dangerous tendency.

    I learned the danger of overconfidence in self in a very painful way when I was in high school. At that time, I was part of a football team that had had an undefeated season in my sophomore, in my junior, and ten games into my senior year. As we came to our eleventh game of the season, we had a winning streak of twenty-seven games. And for this eleventh game, we were preparing to play a team that had already lost to a team that we had defeated easily and badly.

    We came to this game thinking that it was going to be a walk in the park. We figured that the other team might as well not even show up. We were sure that there was no chance in the world that they could ever beat us. After all, we had one of the longest winning streaks that had ever been run up in our state. How could we lose? In our minds, the season was all wrapped up and we had it made.

By now, it is probably obvious what happened during that twenty-eighth game. We lost, and lost badly. Why? One reason, perhaps the main reason, was that we had overestimated ourselves; we were over-confident about our abilities and we had underestimated the power of our opponents.

That is what Peter did as well. Jesus had said to him, "Simon, Simon, behold, Satan has demanded permission to sift you like wheat" (Luke 22:31). Peter replied, "Lord, with You I am ready to go both to prison and to death!" (22:33). Clearly, Peter was over-confident concerning his own strength and seriously underestimated the power of the devil. Peter ignored Christ's warning and the teaching of passages like Proverbs 16:18, which says, "Pride goes before destruction, and a haughty spirit before stumbling."

Peter did not seem to recognize, nor was he concerned about, his own weaknesses. Peter was trusting in himself rather than the Lord. His eyes were on himself and not on the Lord. Peter's overconfidence (pride, really) in himself was certainly one of the main factors in his failure.

11. Before we finish our examination of Peter's failure, there is one other factor that we must not overlook. Careful study of what happened to Peter and why it happened indicates that his failure to put sin to death may have been related to a lack of prayer.

Matthew 26 tells us that when Jesus went with Peter, James, and John into the garden of Gethsemane on the evening before he was to be put on trial, Jesus asked them to "remain here and keep watch with Me" (26:38). Then, having said that, Jesus went away to pray. After a time, He returned to find Peter and the others sleeping instead of praying. Jesus awoke them and admonished them, "Keep watching and praying that you may not enter into temptation" (26:41). Again He went away to pray. When He returned a second time, He found them asleep once again instead of in prayer.

Jesus had clearly told them that if they wanted to avoid giving in to temptation, they must both watch and pray. From what we are told in Matthew 26, it seems clear that Peter, prior to his failure, was remiss in both of these areas. Peter failed to put sin to death on this occasion because he had not been watchful or prayerful. Instead of watching, he slept; instead of praying, he indulged the flesh. His lack of watchfulness was certainly an indication of his failure to see the seriousness of the situation. His prayerlessness surely revealed his self-confidence—his lack of any sense of his need for God's help.

If we want to overcome sin in our lives, there can be no substitute for believing prayer. We absolutely must watch and pray or we will succumb to temptation. Watchfulness and prayerfulness are necessary for victory. Take your concordance sometime and look at how many times this idea of watching and praying go together. Colossians 4:2 exhorts, "Devote yourselves to prayer, keeping alert in it with an attitude of thanksgiving." 1 Peter 4:7 instructs, "The end of all things is near; therefore, be of sound judgment and sober spirit for the purpose of prayer." Ephesians 6:18 teaches, "With all prayer and petition pray at all times in the Spirit, and with this in view, be on the alert with all perseverance and petition for all the saints." Nehemiah 4:9 says, "But we prayed to our God, and because of them we set up a guard against them day and night."

What is the connection between prayer and victory over sin? First, prayer is the God-appointed means of acknowledging our helplessness before God. Jesus told Peter, "Satan wants you, so you had better watch and pray." But Peter did not see his helplessness. He did not think things were as bad as Jesus said they were.

This is often the case with us as well. We do not really think that things in our lives are as bad as Jesus, in His Word, says they are. Otherwise, we would be praying more. We would be constantly acknowledging our helplessness before God. And this failure is due to unbelief. We do not really believe what the Lord says about our enemies, our situations, or ourselves.

Our failure to pray is also one of the greatest evidences of our pride. It is not necessary for us to strut around with our heads in the air to prove that we are proud. All we have to do to reveal our pride is to fail to pray. A prayerless person is a proud person. A prayerless person says to Almighty God, "I am not as bad or as weak and helpless as You say I am. I can get along without You. I can gain victory over my sinful desires and deeds—even over the devil—all by myself." In contrast, a prayerful person is a humble person who comes before God and freely admits that without Him, he can do nothing. He recognizes that he is powerless against his sinful desires and against the devil.

A humble, prayerful person says to God, "Lord, I agree with You that in my flesh there dwells no good thing. I agree with You that the temptations that come from inside and outside of me are too much for me. I desperately need Your help. Lord, I can't even cope with the deceitfulness of my own heart. Sometimes when I think I am being honest, my sinful heart is deceiving me. O God, I am helpless without You. I can do nothing good apart from Your grace. Please help me." We all need to come to the place where we can pray this kind of truly sorrowful prayer to God about our depravity and helplessness.

The second connection between prayer and victory over sin is that prayer is also the God-appointed means of appropriating the Spirit's enablement. In Philippians 1:19, the apostle Paul wrote, "For I know that this will turn out for my deliverance through your prayers and the provision of the Spirit of Jesus Christ." In this passage, Paul made a connection between prayer and the supply of the Holy Spirit. In other words, Paul said that we receive the supply of the Spirit of Jesus Christ by means of prayer. Jesus made the same connection in Luke 11:13: "how much more will your heavenly Father give the Holy Spirit to those who ask Him?"

In prayer we reach out the hand of faith to God and say, "O God, give me the power of the Holy Spirit to overcome these evil desires, these evil urges." In prayer we look to Jesus Christ, the Author and Finisher of our faith, and ask Him to give us the enabling power of the Holy Spirit. At least in part, it seems that Peter's failure had something to do with his lack of prayer. And so it is with many of us; we fail to pray as we ought, and thus we lack the supply of the Spirit of Jesus Christ, Who is an absolute necessity if we are going to kill the sin that is within us.

Do we want victory over temptation? Do we truly desire to mortify sin in our lives? If so, then we must settle in our minds once and for all that if we are going to have victory over evil desires, we must watch and pray. Whether we like it or not, we are going to face the same kinds of problems that Peter faced. And like Peter, we will be tempted to be complacent at times. When that happens, we must steadfastly refuse to give in or give up. If we fail, we will surely be defeated as Peter was.

Watch against Satan! He and his wicked angels are constantly at work, trying to bring believers down. We may not be directly aware of their presence or activity, but they are constantly around to tempt us. Wherever we go, we may be sure that they are there also (1 Peter 5:8). Watch for them!

We also need to watch because the world is just as determined to bring us down. We must guard our hearts against the temptations that come from the fleeting pleasures of this world (Rom. 12:2). And we must watch against our own evil desires that are holdovers from our pre-Christian life. To some degree, they will always remain with us while we are yet on the earth, seeking to lead us into sin.

Watch and pray. Christ's exhortation is as critical and relevant to us today as it was to His disciples in the garden. We must daily acknowledge our helplessness before God, asking Him for His help and the supply of the Spirit of Christ Jesus. Our days should begin thus: "O God, I am not sufficient. Lord, wherever I go and in whatever I do today, I want to be a testimony for You. I want to think, desire, feel, and act in a righteous manner. I want to be delivered from evil and overcome temptation. I need the enablement of Your Spirit to live this day for You and to put my sinful desires to death."

What kind of private prayer life do we have? What kind of private time do we have alone with God? Do we wrestle and agonize in prayer with the Lord? I am convinced that one of the reasons we do not see more power in our lives today is that very few of us as Christians really know what it means to watch and pray. We will never know true victory until we learn to do that.

In Matthew 26, we learn that Peter and the other disciples eventually woke up from their nap in the garden. And what happened to Peter next is a picture of what is happening in our lives and churches today. As soldiers attempted to arrest Jesus, Peter drew his sword and began to wave it around. In his frantic attempt to do what he thought was good, he only made things worse. Instead of protecting Christ, all he managed to do was to slice off a servant's ear. As Peter tried to live and serve in his own strength, he only made a mess. He waved his arms around and was determined to do something for God, and yet he accomplished nothing.

That same thing is happening in many of our lives and many of our churches today. There is much activity, but very little is really happening for God's kingdom. All too often, our lives as Christians are not all that different from the lives of unbelievers around us. We think the way they think, we talk the way they talk, we desire the same things they desire, we act and react the way they do, and we value the same things they value. Instead of putting sin to death, we excuse it, indulge it, and think lightly of it.

Sadly, some professing Christians do not seem to mind living this way, saying, "So what? If I yield to the desires and deeds of the flesh in any of the ways described in Colossians 3:5–11 and other passages, I can't do anything about it. I keep thinking and talking and desiring and acting in ways that are displeasing to God, but victory doesn't seem possible. For me, there is no way I can be an overcomer. I just can't kill my sin in the way that Paul says I should."

My fellow Christian, we may be sure that if we have a sin problem that is constantly harassing us, there is victory. We can be overcomers. There is a way to conquer sinful desires. We must remember what the Bible says about putting sin to death and about not fulfilling the desires of the flesh (Gal. 5:16–26). We must remember that when God's Word encourages us to put sin to death, it means, of course, that as believers we can do what it says. We must remember God's promise that if we put sin to death in our lives, we will then experience real life. Finally, we must also remember the warning of Scripture that if we do not destroy the deeds of the body, we will be destroyed by our sin. It is kill or be killed.

As suggested in the introduction to this book, let all of us as Christians involve ourselves in the exterminating business. With God's help, let us devote ourselves to putting the suggestions of this book into practice and get serious about killing our sin so that we may live wisely, righteously, joyfully, fruitfully, and godly in this present world.

APPLICATION AND DISCUSSION SUGGESTIONS

1. List the things mentioned in this chapter that we should do to help us put Romans 8:13 and Colossians 3:5–9 into practice in our lives.

2. List the Scriptures that support the importance of doing the things mentioned in this chapter if we want to actually fulfill the commands of Romans 8:13 and Colossians 3:5.

3. What were the characteristics of Peter's failure as described in this chapter?

4. What can we learn from this that may be helpful to us in putting our sin to death?

5. What can we learn from the experience of Peter when he failed to put sin to death as described in this chapter? Describe what happened on this occasion.

6. What are some of the probable reasons for Peter's failure?

7. List all the ideas presented in this book about why sin is so serious.

8. Why is prayer such an important part of putting Romans 8:13 and Colossians 3:5 into practice in our lives?

9. What does prayerlessness indicate?

10. List all the ideas presented in this book about what we should do to help us put Romans 8:13 and Colossians 3:5 into practice.

11. Why is a failure to practice Romans 8:13 and Colossians 3:5 a serious matter?

12. Do you regularly carry out the sin-killing practices described in this chapter? Try to identify specific examples of times that you did. Be ready to share them with your discussion group or counselor.

13. What practical applications for your Christian life will you make from this chapter and from the entire book?

NOTES

Chapter 1: Think about This

1. Charles Spurgeon, "Man's Depravity." Quoted in A.W. Pink, "The Christian in Romans 7," www.pbministries.org/books/pink/Miscellaneous/romans_7.htm (accessed October 5, 2005).

Chapter 2: Know Your Enemy

1. Cornelius Plantinga Jr., *Not the Way It's Supposed to Be: A Breviary of Sin* (Grand Rapids: Eerdmans, 1995), 105.

2. Thomas Watson, *The Doctrine of Repentance* (Edinburgh: Banner of Truth, 1999), 112.

Chapter 3: The World's Worst Tyrant

1. Ralph Venning, *The Sinfulness of Sin* (Edinburgh, Scotland: Banner of Truth, 1997).

2. Ibid.

3. Al Martin, "Practical Helps to Mortification of Sin," *Banner of Truth* 106 (n.d.): 30.

4. Charles Spurgeon, "Sin Slain," 1860, www.biblebb.com/files/spurgeon/0337.html (accessed August 28, 2005).

Chapter 4: Dumb and Dumber

1. For powerful illustrations of the stupidity of sin see Cornelius Platinga Jr., *Not the Way It's Supposed to Be: A Breviary of Sin* (Grand Rapids: Eerdmans, 1995). This book is a great resource on what makes sin so evil.

2. Ibid., 121, 123.

Chapter 5: If It's So Bad, Why Do I Feel So Good?

1. John MacArthur, "Hell—The Furnace of Fire," www.biblebb.com/files/MAC/sg2304.html (accessed August 28, 2005).

2. In the following section I owe much to a sermon preached by John Piper, "Unless You Repent You Will All Likewise Perish," www.desiringgod.org/library/sermons/88/060588.html (accessed August 28, 2005).

3. Ibid.

4. Ibid.

5. Robert Murray McCheyne, "The Hell of the Bible Is Not Annihilation," http://biblestudyplanet.com/s90.htm (accessed October 5, 2005).

Chapter 6: What Killing Your Sin Means

1. Jerry Bridges, *The Gospel for Real Life* (Colorado Springs: NavPress, 2003), 178–79.

Chapter 7: You Can Kill Your Sin Because . . .

1. Wayne Mack and Joshua Mack, *God's Solutions to Life's Problems* (Tulsa, OK: Hensley Publishing, 2002), 184.

2. John Owen, *The Works of John Owen*, vol. 3 (London: Banner of Truth, 1966), 471.

3. Adapted from Wayne Mack and Joshua Mack, *God's Solutions to Life's Problems* (Tulsa, OK: Hensley Publishing, 2002), 187–89.

4. Adapted from ibid., 217.

5. Adapted from ibid., 226–27.

Chapter 8: Remember, You Don't Sin Alone

1. William Hendricksen, *The New Testament Commentary* (Grand Rapids: Baker, 1967), 381–82.

Chapter 9: Pay Attention to the Seasons

1. William Hendricksen, *The New Testament Commentary* (Grand Rapids: Baker, 1967), 232–33.

2. Ibid., 233–34.

3. Johann Freystein, *Trinity Hymnal* (Philadelphia: Great Commission Publications, 1961), no. 476, vv. 1–4.

Chapter 10: You Must Know Yourself

1. John Bunyan, *The Pilgrim's Progress*, Cheryl Ford trans. (Wheaton, IL: Tyndale, 1991), 80.

2. John Owen, *The Works of John Owen*, vol. 6 (Edinburgh: Banner of Truth, 1966), 132–33.

3. Quoted by Charles Spurgeon in *Treasury of David* (Byron Center, MI: Associated Publishers, 1970), 153–54.

4. Ibid., 154.

INDEX OF SCRIPTURE

Genesis
2:15–17—93
3—93, 133, 140, 142
3:6—93, 134
4—139, 140
8:21—87
12—139
20—139
26—139
27—139, 140
37—139
39—139

Exodus
34:7—95

Numbers
14—152

Joshua
1:8–9—148
6—146
7—146

2 Samuel
11—153
11:1–2—112
12—153
12:13–14—90

1 Kings
18—112, 152
19—151, 152

Nehemiah
4:9—164

Job
1—142
1:14–19—134–35
1:20–22—136
2—136, 142
2:7–9—136
2:10—137
4:3–4—94

Psalms
1:1—103
1:2–3—148

10:4—103
11:6—54
32:3–4—40
36:9—105
51:4—27
58:3—139
97:10—17
119:45—11
119:59—148
119:59–60—125, 130
119:67—108
119:105—105
119:128—128
141:3—138

Proverbs
1:7—103
1:10—101
1:15—101
1:29–32—108
4:26—94
5:3–8—101
6:6–11—99
6:23—105
7—96

8:13—52
9:10—103
11:2—40
13:15—47
14:9—14, 42, 47
14:12—127
14:15–16—120
14:16—47
16:2—127
16:18—162
17:14—142
18:13—129
18:15—129
18:21—138
19:19—118
22:24–25—40
26:11—35
26:16—119
26:23–25—120
29:5—120
30:7–9—109

Ecclesiastes
9:3—87
12:13—103

Isaiah
35:3–4—95

Jeremiah
4:22—45
17:9—25, 86, 116

Ezekiel
16:15—29
36:26—77

Zechariah
3:3—35
4:6—82

Malachi
2:15–17—140

Matthew
1:21—89
5:13–16—106
5:14–26—105
5:27–30—9
5:30—54
7:24—45
7:26—45
8:12—55
13:41–42—55
16:21–23—160
17:1–13—160
22:13—55
23:27–28—35
25:30—55
25:41—55
26—154, 155, 158,
    159, 162, 163, 167
26:30–75—154
26:31—155
26:33—155
26:35—155
26:38—163
26:41—96, 104, 163
26:69–75—156
26:70—157
26:72—157
26:74—157

Mark
7:21—86
7:21–23—88, 116,
    128, 130, 140
9—113
9:5—113
9:43–47—102, 104,
    108
10:23–25—109

Luke
9—118
9:54—118
11:13—165
12:17–19—46
12:20–21—46
12:48—111
13—57–58, 62, 65
13:2—58
13:3—59
13:4–5—58
13:5—59, 61
18—117
18:11–12—117
21:34—108
22—156
22:31—162
22:33—162
22:46—114
22:61–62—157

John
1:4–5—105
1:9—105
3:16—62
3:19–21—105
5:35—105
8:12—105
16:8–9—85
16:14—85
17:15–18—106
21:15–19—158

Acts
1:8—85
5—140
10:9–16—158
20:28–31—97
20:30–31—97
26:18—77

Romans
1:18—139
1:18–23—43–44
1:18–25—50
1:25—139
2:12—62
3:9–18—139
3:10–18—86
3:24–25—14
5:12—93
6:12—78
6:14—78
6:23—33
7:18—88
8:2—83
8:2–4—85
8:7—87
8:11–13—83
8:13—9, 13, 69, 78,
    80, 81, 84, 90, 91,
    98, 103, 104, 141,
    142, 145, 152, 155,
    168, 169
8:26—85
8:29—144, 145
12:1–2—10
12:2—166
13:12—105
13:14—36
15:4—150

1 Corinthians
2:14–16—85
5:1–12—93
5:2–5—94
5:6–7—93
6:11—85
10:1–11—152
10:5—150
10:11—150
13:4–8—138

15:9—20
15:34—99
16:13–14—81
16:13—76

2 Corinthians
3:18—85
5:14–15—92
7:1—70
7:1–9—121
7:9–11—158
10:4–5—138
11:14—105
13:5—116
13:14—85

Galatians
2:11–14—158
5:16—83, 84
5:16–26—168
5:19–21—128, 130
5:22–23—85
6:7–8—34, 41

Ephesians
1:7—14
2:3—88
2:8–9—14
2:10—14
3:8—20
3:16–18—85
4:14—120
4:17—28
4:17–19—43, 52
4:25—141
4:25–32—82, 106
4:26–27—38
4:29—138
4:30—82, 85
5:3—106
5:4—106

5:9—107
5:11—105, 106, 159
5:25–26—89
6:10–13—75
6:18—164

Philippians
1:19—165
2:12—70
2:12–13—69
3:12—144, 145
3:12–14—73, 81
3:13—146
3:14—145
4:8—138

Colossians
1:21–23—87
3:1–9—71
3:1–4—81
3:5—9, 13, 69, 71, 74,
    80, 81, 98, 104,
    141, 142, 145, 152,
    155, 169
3:5–9—90, 91, 103,
    141, 152, 168
3:5–11—167
3:6—13, 51
3:8—72, 76
3:9—72, 90, 140, 141,
    142
4:2—163

1 Thessalonians
5:19—82

2 Thessalonians
1:7–9—54

1 Timothy
1:7—85

1:15—20, 73
4:7–9—10
5:22—40
6:12—75

2 Timothy
2:3–4—81
2:3–5—76
3:1–6—128, 130

Titus
2:7–11—14
2:12—88
2:14—14, 86, 89, 90
3:5–6—14
3:8—14

Hebrews
7:26—145
9:14—88
10:29—55

12:1—38, 95
12:12–13—94
12:14–15—95

James
1:6—120
1:12–15—9
1:13–15—142
1:17—105

1 Peter—158
1:13–16—10
2:1–2—40
2:11—40, 76, 78, 81
2:24—86
3:7—40
4:7—163
5:8—97, 166

2 Peter—158
1:5–11—11

1 John
1:5—105
1:7—105
1:8–10—73
2:9–10—105
3:4—24, 26
4:9–11—92
4:19—92

3 John
9–10—117

Jude
12—120

Revelation
3:17–18—110
20:15—54

Wayne A. Mack (M.Div., Philadelphia Theological Seminary; D.Min., Westminster Theological Seminary) serves Christ and His church as Professor of biblical counseling for eight months out of the year at a pastoral training institute in South Africa, where he also conducts conferences and seminars. For the remaining four months out of the year, he and his wife return to the United States to teach at a pastoral training institute sponsored by the Bible Church of Little Rock, Arkansas.

Wayne is adjunct professor of biblical counseling at The Master's College and director of Strengthening Ministries International. He is an executive board member of F.I.R.E. (Fellowship of Independent Reformed Evangelicals), and a charter member and executive board member of the National Association of Nouthetic Counselors. Wayne is also a member of the board of directors of the missionary agency Publicacione Fara de Gracia.

Mack has authored a number of books, including *Down, but Not Out*; *Humility*; *Reaching the Ear of God*; *Strengthening Your Marriage*; *Your Family, God's Way*. He and his wife, Carol, have four children and thirteen grandchildren.

Joshua Mack (M.A. in Biblical Counseling, The Master's College; M.Div. The Master's Seminary) is pastor of Grace Fellowship Church in Pennsylvania's Lehigh Valley. He is the co-author of *The Fear Factor* and *God's Solutions to Life's Problems*. Mack and his wife, Marda, live in the Lehigh Valley with their three daughters. To read more of Joshua Mack's writings, visit his blog at www.joshmack.blogspot.com.

About Strengthening Ministries International

Strengthening Ministries International provides training and resources to strengthen you and your church. We exist to glorify God by doing what Paul and his associates did in Acts 14:21–22. They went about preaching the gospel, making disciples, strengthening the souls of those disciples, and encouraging them to continue in the faith.

Like Paul, we are dedicated to using whatever gifts and abilities, training and experience, resources and opportunities we have to strengthen Christians and churches in their commitment to Christ and in their ministries for Christ.

Fulfilling our ministry involves conducting seminars and conferences across the United States and internationally. It includes writing and distributing books, as well as developing and distributing audio and videotapes on numerous biblical, theological, and counseling subjects.

Fulfilling our purpose also includes developing and sustaining our web site: www.mackministries.org. There you can find fuller descriptions of the various aspects of our ministry.

Strengthening Ministries International
Resource Administrator: Charles Busby
P.O. Box 1656
Lacombe, LA 70445-1656
Phone: 985-882-3342
(Faxes can be received if you call this number first)
email: webmaster@mackministries.org